Manage Your Time

Sally Garratt became an indep
gaining considerable work ex
industry and with design practices. She first travelled to East
Asia in 1976 and is now a director of a strategy consultancy
based in Hong Kong. She has worked with her husband on
assignments relating to strategy and organizational change
in Hong Kong, Australia, New Zealand and the UK. She has
designed and run development programmes for senior
professional and executive women, training courses in
personal effectiveness/time management and interviewing
skills, and worked with sixthformers on 'insight into industry' and 'challenge of management' courses. She has also
written sales training programmes and carried out research
for television programmes and the construction industry.

She has a degree in Malay and Anthropology from
London University and is a member of the Institute of
Personnel Management and the Association for Manage-
ment Education and Development.

Bob Garratt is a company director, consultant and academic.
He is Chairman of Media Projects International in London
and of Organization Development Limited in Hong Kong.
He consults in director development and the development of
strategic thinking in Europe, Asia, Australia, New Zealand,
and the USA. He is Visiting Fellow at the Management
School of Imperial College, London University, an Associate
of the Judge Institute of Management, Cambridge University
and immediate past Chairman of the Association for Management Education and Development.

Other titles in the Successful Strategist series:

Titles in the Successful Manager series:

Sally Garratt

Manage Your Time

■ HarperCollins*Publishers*

HarperCollins*Publishers*,
77–85 Fulham Palace Road,
Hammersmith, London W6 8JB

This revised paperback edition 1994
1 3 5 7 9 8 6 4 2

Previously published in paperback by Fontana 1985
Reprinted 6 times

First published simultaneously in hardback by Collins 1985

ISBN 0 00 638411 0

Set in Linotron Palatino and Frutiger by
Hewer Text Composition Services, Edinburgh

Printed in Great Britain by
HarperCollinsManufacturing, Glasgow

CONTENTS

PREFACE

When I first wrote this book in 1985, I would not have dared to predict that I would be revising and updating it nine years later. Since working with more organizations and individuals, I've developed my ideas and realized that the whole subject is more than just the management of time. It's really about Personal Effectiveness, of which time management is a part. That is why I've expanded some of the existing paragraphs. The original book concentrated on conventional 'work' in conventional workplaces. Additions will embrace the increasingly common different ways of working and include more about 'out of work' activities. They will also cover aspects of you as an individual and your ability to cope with the pressures and demands of your everyday life.

Why a book on time management?

'He who controls others may be powerful, but he who has mastered himself is mightier still,' wrote Lao Tsu. In his book *The Effective Manager*, Peter Drucker points out that 'The supply of time is totally inelastic. Time is totally perishable and cannot be stored. Time is totally irreplaceable . . . there is no substitute for time.' The Mad Hatter in *Alice in Wonderland* says, 'If you knew Time as well as I do, you wouldn't talk about wasting it. I daresay you never even spoke to Time. Now if you only kept on good terms with him, he'd do anything you liked with the clock.'

Most managers find that they do not have enough time during a day to carry out all the tasks that they see as essential to their jobs. However, a great deal of time is wasted on activities that are unproductive and managers are constantly aware of demands on their time which contribute little or nothing to the effective accomplishment of the main objectives of their jobs.

I had been vaguely aware of this problem in the realm of office work since 1964 when, as a newly qualified secretary, I began working for a professional association and soon discovered that the bosses there did not make the best use of their support staff, especially the secretaries. During my second job, as personal assistant to one of the architect partners in a large multi-disciplinary practice, I discovered the satisfaction of being given increasingly responsible tasks to do and soon realized how rare is the boss who can delegate effectively, particularly when I looked around the organization and saw other secretaries' talents and time being sadly wasted. This boss has since admitted that, far from knowing how to delegate well, he just threw everything at me because 'you seemed to be able to cope'. In my naivety, I thought this was the way things were done! Anyway, in this case it worked and we both learned a great deal.

When I became a boss, it grew frighteningly clear to me how difficult it is to be an effective manager of time. I knew what I wanted my secretary to do because I knew what I had been able to accomplish in a similar role, but there suddenly seemed so much more to do in a day, so many important and urgent tasks to get finished in next to no time, and so many deadlines to meet. I know I failed this vital test of management and I began to realize why I, and thousands of other managers, do not manage our time effectively.

For a start, you are rarely helped to deal with the changes demanded of you when you become a manager for the first time or when you take on new roles within a management team. The ability to manage people, new responsibilities, an unfamiliar workload and different terms of reference does not automatically appear, as if by divine intervention, as soon as you become a manager. I'm sure many of you will recognize and remember the frustrations because no one offers any practical guidance when you take on managerial responsibilities. It is a sensitive area which many managers choose to ignore because it is easier to do that than to face up to the painful process of organizing the way they work.

This book is designed to give some of that help. The examples are practical – I have included only those hints and techniques which I know work from personal experience.

If you are looking at this book, it probably means that you realize there is a problem but you don't know how to go about solving it. I can't promise to answer all your questions but I hope you'll be able to find ways round some of the difficulties. If you are prepared to help yourself, I'll be delighted if somewhere in the book you discover the way to do this, or find out where you can get the help you need.

I have tried to avoid using the singular he/she, his/her, him/her wherever possible, simply to make the text easier to read. It is a fact that most managers in this country are still men, so where I have had to differentiate between a manager and, for example, a secretary, I have made the manager a man and the secretary a woman, thus reflecting the current situation.

There does appear to be an increase in the number of senior managers and directors who are women. My impression is that, in the latter half of the eighties, there were a number of senior women managers who belonged to the 'I got where I am without any help so other women will have to do the same' school. That attitude is, I hope and believe, changing to a more helpful one which says, 'I want to help women achieve their rightful place at work and I will play my part as mentor, role model, whatever is needed.' There are, I am delighted to say, some very good women executives in the making in all types of working environment.

9

Introduction: recognizing the real problem

The first thing to do is to admit that you do have a problem in managing your time.

'I don't have the time' may be an excuse that comes readily to the tongue but next time you hear yourself saying it, stop for a moment and consider the truth of that statement. Do you really not have enough time or are you saying it out of habit?

The second thing you have to admit is that this lack of time is often your fault. It's so easy to blame everybody else for the fact that you have to take work home at night, that you miss deadlines, that the day's work is never planned, that you end up doing everything yourself because nobody else can do it, and that you never have time to prepare for all those meetings (which are a waste of time anyway). As for home life and social events . . . well, you can forget those because work is more important, isn't it?

You can convince yourself that the reason other people cope better than you do is because your job is different, more demanding, and your staff aren't of the right quality or quantity to give you adequate support. Even if you do acknowledge that you would benefit from organizing yourself better, you know it will take a lot of time to do that, and time is the one thing that you don't have enough of.

11

If you are unorganized, then your staff (if you have any) will also be unorganized and the resulting chaos leads to confusion, misunderstanding and a dissatisfied collection of individuals unable to operate as a team.

If you are unorganized, then your boss will not be able to recommend you for advancement within the organization, and your peers will see that you are not to be relied on to come up with the goods on time or of the appropriate quality. This puts a great strain on your relationships with the people you work with at all levels.

If you are unorganized, you will have to spend more and more time at work or doing work at home. If you have other demands on your time from family or friends or social and leisure activities, you will feel the pressure building up as you keep saying 'No' or 'Not just now' or 'I'm sorry, I must do this work'. If, as a sole trader or self-employed person, you are unorganized, you will soon find yourself without work. Clients, whether internal or external, expect their suppliers to be efficient and effective and, in the current economic situation, there is no shortage of people ready to take your place. If you have moved from being employed by someone else to becoming self-employed, you will soon recognize that you have to become a generalist, managing all aspects of the business, and this is a far cry from the specialist role that most managers have had to play in traditional organizations.

During the current employment situation, particularly, managers are aware that they must do their jobs well if they are to keep them. Middle managers in particular are aware that they are increasingly under threat and they know they must bring extra value to their jobs if they are to keep them. As most managers have not received any formal management training, they think that doing their job well means spending a lot of time doing it. Indeed, the culture of some companies encourages the myth that the more time you spend working, the more you achieve and the better you are at doing your job.

It is vital to get the balance right between the parts of your life that are important to you, and only when you recognize what that balance is can you get work into perspective. If you want to pursue this further, it is covered in more detail in the section 'What do I want?' I firmly believe that most of us work more effectively if we have found this balance. It will vary according to the individual, so it is up to you to search for the right balance for you.

It takes a lot of courage to face up to the fact that you are going to have to work very hard at managing your time more effectively. Trying to implement all your good intentions means investing time now to reap the benefits later on so other people – your family, friends and colleagues – are also going to be affected and they may not enjoy the experience as you make your first steps towards becoming organized.

Don't be discouraged by the size of the task ahead of you. It may seem enormous but, luckily, it can be tackled one step at a time. If you try to do everything at once you will fail, but as you take things steadily, gradually trying out new ways of organizing yourself and your team, you will be encouraged by your success. People around you will be so impressed by the new organized you that they will try and emulate you, especially as they will look increasingly more chaotic in comparison with you.

Good luck. Enjoy the challenge and look forward to a more organized future where you are in control.

How do you manage your time?

Time management means a lot of things. It is one of those subjects which can cover a huge area and it is quite possible that this book includes things you don't think of as falling under that heading, or may have left out others that you think are basic time management problems. However, as most management matters are interrelated, those areas which are not covered here will almost certainly be mentioned in other books in this series.

The following list asks questions about subjects that will be covered in this book. Please delete 'Yes' or 'No' as appropriate.

Do you:

1 tackle the most difficult tasks early in the morning?   Yes/No

2 write a list of 'things that must be done today'?   Yes/No

3 ever say 'No' when asked to do something?   Yes/No

4 ever ask 'Why' when invited to go to a meeting?   Yes/No

5 think that managers and executives above you waste less time than you do?   Yes/No

6 give priority to matters which are urgent, rather than to those which are important?   Yes/No

7 put all tasks into priority order and work on them in that order?   Yes/No

8 tackle one task at a time, finish it and then move on to the next one?   Yes/No

9 accept all unscheduled interruptions?   Yes/No

10	keep paperwork for meetings down to a minimum?	Yes/No
11	regularly take work home in the evening or at weekends?	Yes/No
12	prefer doing things yourself rather than give them to members of your staff?	Yes/No
13	ever dictate to a secretary or into an audio machine?	Yes/No
14	talk to your boss about the everyday events at work?	Yes/No
15	discuss your work with your secretary?	Yes/No
16	ask other people how they organize their time?	Yes/No
17	ever leave the building to work elsewhere if you have something important to do?	Yes/No
18	wish you could type?	Yes/No
19	recruit your own staff?	Yes/No
20	ever think about the issues raised by these questions?	Yes/No

The maddening thing about a list of questions like the ones above is that they don't have clear-cut answers. You've probably added a rider to each one. For instance, 'I do try and tackle one thing at a time and finish it before I go on to the next job, but something else always crops up that I've got to see to immediately' or 'I know I should say "No" more often, but I'm worried about what will happen to me if I refuse to take on everything I'm asked to do' or 'I do take quite a lot of work home. I can't do it at the office because of all the interruptions.'

From recent discussions with many managers, I have found that those who manage their time best answer 'Yes' to most of those questions. Let's look at some of them in more detail.

Some of the questions depend so much on the individual that it is impossible to be dogmatic about the answer. Question 1, for example, does not apply to everybody. I know I work well first thing in the morning but many of my close colleagues are hopeless until their third cup of coffee, so I can achieve a great deal while they are still coming to terms with a new day.

You may well think that those managers and executives mentioned in Question 5 waste just as much time as you do. They shouldn't, because they have greater opportunity than you to use their time effectively. They have access to more resources, for example, but that doesn't necessarily mean that they are using them properly. If you have criticized those above you for wasting time, think about what your subordinates say about you. Is it possible that they are accusing you of the same things? You could ask them – but only if you are prepared to listen to honest, perhaps unpalatable answers. You can learn a lot from talking to those people who work with and for you.

Question 6 is about dividing tasks into those which are urgent and those which are important. This is covered in greater detail later on because most of us don't consciously see these as two different issues. There are times when a small urgent task may be dealt with immediately, just to get it out of the way, but there is a danger of sorting out all the small urgent tasks only to find that the day has passed you by and you are still left with the important things to do.

Unscheduled interruptions are mentioned by most managers as being one of the greatest hindrances to effective working. It is almost impossible to ignore them all and, anyway, it could be something important so you have to assess the worth of each one. Most people don't want to appear rude or uninterested, but there are ways of discouraging the nuisance visitor or unimportant interruption.

One of the greatest timewasters at work today is the meeting. Properly scheduled and organized, they can be enormously useful but so often the small benefits do not warrant the time, effort and cost spent on them. Supporting paperwork for meetings must be relevant to the matter in hand and sent out in good time, but careful attention should be paid to the wording and content of agendas.

It is tempting to leave the 'thinking' work until you have a chance to sit down, without interruptions, for longer than half an hour and that is why so many managers regularly take work home. How often, though, does it stay in the briefcase because, by the time you've had supper, you're too tired to do anything more than slump down and ponder on the amount of work you have to do? It also means that you're so busy worrying about the work you're not doing that you miss out on the other side of life, whether it is family, sport or some other leisure activity.

Newly promoted managers are keen to show how good they are at their jobs. They want to prove that they can do everything that their subordinates do. However, if you take on everything that is pushed your way and insist on doing it yourself, you will soon disappear under a pile of paper and good intentions. Your staff are there to help you, to work with you and part of your job is to help them develop. It is worth investing time now to delegate work to them, so that you may get on with the new, challenging job that you have taken on. It is not only your staff who can help you. It is often most rewarding to establish good working relations with your peers both inside and outside the organization. Good turns certainly deserve another and co-operation between colleagues can prove mutually beneficial.

These issues, and those raised by the remaining questions

which are generally answered 'Yes' by successful managers of time, will all be covered in the following pages.

The different sections of this book will attempt to help you overcome some of the worries you have about managing your time. Questions like the ones in the list above will, I hope, start you thinking about the ways in which you can begin to organize yourself and others. Have you ever, for example, really thought about when you work best? Are you a lark or an owl? Or are you, like me, good for nothing for an hour in the early afternoon? Each of us is different and if you have a best time, when your mind is at its most active and creative, you should try to tackle all the difficult tasks, the planning, analyses, thinking, during that period. Your not-so-good time could be used for tasks that aren't so demanding, small jobs that can be finished off quickly without a great deal of effort.

Look at the following two studies, and think which one reflects the way you work at present. Be honest. If you fool yourself now, you won't be able to recognize the areas where you can begin to change your work pattern and make yourself a more effective manager.

STUDY 1

Frank Bishop had recently been promoted to manager of a small department in an engineering firm. An electrical engineer by profession, he had spent most of his time designing and overseeing the installation of systems. The new job meant that he now had to manage fifteen people and make sure that they carried out the sort of work he used to do.

He took over from a man who moved to a more senior position within the company but on a different site, and the changeover period had only been a month. Frank hadn't been able to learn much from his predecessor because he had been too occupied in sorting out his own move to the new job. Never having had any management training, right from the start he had felt completely out of his depth.

He spent a great deal of time checking that his staff were doing their job properly. This meant that to get through all the paperwork he was coming in at eight o'clock in the morning and not leaving until past seven in the evening. He also began to take work home at night and at weekends, and later on he started coming into the office on Saturdays to clear the backlog.

When he wasn't watching his staff, he had to go to meetings which seemed to him to go on for ever without achieving anything. The phone never seemed to stop ringing nor people continuously popping in for a chat. He hadn't seen his boss for more than a few minutes at a time and, after three months, he was beginning to feel really fed up about the situation.

It all came out in the open the other day when one of the men he used to work with was passing by his office and was surprised to see Frank slumped in his chair, head in his hands, and looking thoroughly miserable. 'What on earth's the matter, Frank?' he asked. 'You look dreadful. I thought you would be full of the joys of spring having reached the heights of management!'

Frank sighed deeply. 'It's awful', he admitted. 'There aren't enough people to do the work, and those that are there don't seem to be capable of thinking for themselves. My boss is never around, except to demand more from me, with unrealistic deadlines, no resources and even though I'm working round the clock, I don't seem to be getting anywhere. Even my wife's beginning to complain – she just doesn't understand the difficulties I'm facing. I don't seem to be able to rely on anybody at all – none of the other managers appears to be having all this trouble.'

STUDY 2

Jackie Hargreaves was feeling somewhat apprehensive about her new job. She had been a super salesperson and then a successful regional sales manager but she was beginning to feel that, in accepting the promotion to Sales Manager, England and Wales, she might have bitten off more than she could chew.

She knew that she could sell anything to anybody and her sales record had been superb but, if she were honest with herself, there were some things that had happened during her time as regional sales manager that she wasn't completely happy with.

The way the job had seemed to control her rather than the other way round, for example. She had been too proud, or was it scared, to ask her colleagues for help and she knew that her team was becoming discontented with the way she had been organizing things. She never seemed to be able to spend any time with them and the crises used to drain them so they didn't have the energy to give their full attention to the new campaigns.

She knew that, to the outside world, she looked the epitome of the successful young manager, and a woman to boot, but she knew she had made mistakes and she was determined that things would be better in the new job.

The initial sales training she had received with the company had been sound, but rather limited in its scope, and it was becoming obvious that there was more to being a good manager than just being good at the job. She had asked the personnel people to look into general management courses and she was looking forward to seeing what they came up with. She thought it would be good to meet other people in a similar situation as well as being a welcome opportunity to develop herself further.

The first week in the new job had been chaotic even though

Jackie had insisted on spending a month with her predecessor. There were no guidelines as to how the department operated so she had spent some time talking to her new staff, finding out what they did and looking at the job descriptions to try and discover what they should be doing.

She was overawed by the amount of paperwork that kept appearing on her desk. Her secretary, Pat, finally took pity on her and offered some very sound advice on how to deal with it and, as she gradually began to organize that side of the work, Jackie realized that she was more than 'just a typist'. They agreed that a weekly discussion of how work in the office was going would be very useful and that was slotted into the diary as a regular event.

The director, a rather imposing man, seemed determined to offload as much of his work as possible onto Jackie. It became obvious that she couldn't do it all and, anyway, she wasn't even sure that some of the work was her responsibility in the first place.

That made her wonder if she was doing the same to her staff. Was she keeping tasks to herself that they should be doing? Was she giving them work that she should be doing? Was she explaining what she wanted them to do in a way that ensured the end product was the right one?

A lot of time had been spent in meetings and Jackie thought that some of them seemed to be convened more out of habit than anything. She decided to discuss the terms of reference with the other participants to see if the number of meetings could be reduced.

Jackie began to think that things might not be quite as bad as she had first thought. She decided that if she and her staff organized themselves better and worked more effectively as a team, then they should be able to get more done. She also realized that she might be able to leave herself enough time to enrol for the computer appreciation course after all.

CHAPTER 1

What are you there for?

Have you been able to sit back recently and take a cool look at what you are doing at work? Have you thought about the impact you are having on the organization and the people who work for it? Have you looked ahead to how you can help make the company more successful, and you and your staff more fulfilled by the work you are doing? Have you wondered about where the next assignment is coming from when the current one is finished?

The chances are that you haven't had time to allow yourself the luxury of such an examination of what you are doing. This chapter asks you to look at your job to find out why you are doing it, what you should be achieving, and if you are going the right way about it. We'll start with an examination of what you are actually doing.

Keeping a time log

How sure are you about where your time goes during the working week? Could you look back on the past day and given an accurate account of what you did – telephone calls, impromptu chats, unscheduled interruptions, reading reports, answering mail and all the other things that typically constitute a manager's job? It would be very unusual if you could remember everything because so many different and varied activities take place at work.

Figure 1

Time Log	Date
	October 7th 1993

Start time	Activity
0830	
0900	
0930	
1000	
1030	
1100	
1130	
1200	
1230	
1300	
1330	
1400	
1430	
1500	
1530	
1600	
1630	
1700	
1730	

If you really do want to begin to organize yourself, you could start by keeping a log of the tasks you perform during a week. This is a bind, certainly, but only when you know how you are actually spending your time can you make considered judgements about whether you are spending that time on the right things. You can then think about how you *should* be spending your day and decide which tasks take priority.

There are several ways of logging your time and two of these are shown in Figures 1 and 2. You will have to choose which method suits you best, or you may want to devise your own way.

I find that the most useful way of logging time is to jot down every new activity as it happens and note how long that activity has taken. It is important that you fill in activities as they happen, not as you remember them at the end of the day. We don't remember everything and it is usually the minor events we forget to record which are the real time-wasters. You may end up with something that looks like Figure 2. You will probably be horrified at how much time you are spending when dealing with unscheduled interruptions, such as the phone call that you decide to deal with immediately, rather than wait until you have finished your current task, or in speaking to a colleague who is passing by your office and has popped in for a chat. You probably didn't realize how many tasks you started and didn't finish, or how little time you spent on important matters.

Please don't be discouraged by these findings. It probably won't be of much consolation to you that the vast majority of managers has the same difficulties, but you should be cheered by the fact that now you know where the problems are, you should be able to do something about overcoming them.

Figure 2

Time Log		
Start time	**Activity**	**Duration**
0845	Arrive - make coffee	5
0850	Read through day file	10
0900	Telephone call from Dave	2
0902	Day file	5
0907	Chris stops for chat	8
0915	Day file	8
0923	Go to Kay's desk - not there - leave note	7
0930	John asks advice on detail	13
0943	Kay rings - discussion about cladding	6
0949	Penny brings post - chat	6
0955	Go through post	14
1009	Ask Penny to do letter - reply to contractor	9
1018	Continue reading post	12
1030	Ring QS - response to letter	5
1035	Make coffee - chat to Peter	15
1050	Write minutes of site meeting	9
1059	Phone call from tile supplier - argument!	5
1104	Loo	5
1109	Site meeting minutes	16
1125	Charles rings about squash match	5
1130	Site meeting minutes	17
1147	Tile supplier rings	3
1150	Site meeting minutes	7
1157	John asks for more advice	15

etc..

STUDY 3

Diana Bailey had been a secretary in an architectural practice for four years when she was given the chance to move out of secretarial work into a junior managerial post.

She had been studying for membership of the Institute of Personnel Management and her enthusiasm had been recognized by the senior partner, who asked her to become responsible for personnel work within the practice which employed just over two hundred people.

The personnel post was a new one, and she didn't really know what was expected of her, but she felt sure that the job would become clearer as time went on. In the meantime, she did everything she was asked to do by the partners and associates who were only too willing to pass on the difficult problems of the day-to-day running of the practice. There was some difficulty with the younger technical staff, who were still inclined to treat her as a secretary. One or two of the other admin staff reckoned she was getting too big for her boots, so she let it be known that she was still willing to help out if some of the other girls had too much to do, or if one of the partners had some special work that needed doing.

She worked really hard but was never quite sure whether she was doing the right things. She felt that there should be more to what she was doing, that the days were filled with dealing with numerous little tasks, apparently unrelated, and she didn't really see how the new job was so different from the old one.

What she would really like to do is clarify her present job in terms of tasks and areas of responsibility.

What is your job?

Before you can usefully analyse the results of your time log, you should perhaps spend some time looking at your job and what it entails. By that, I don't necessarily mean the things you are currently involved in, but rather the reasons for the job existing at all. Your purpose is to assist the organization to achieve its objectives and it doesn't matter whether you are the office manager, the marketing and sales director, a civil engineer or the works manager – you are there to help the business achieve its goals, to be successful and to make money.

As a first step, look at your job description. ('What?' I hear you cry. 'You must be joking! I've never seen a description for this job.') If you don't have such a document, you should still have a reasonably clear idea of what you were employed to do in the first place. If not, write your own and then ask other people – your boss, your subordinates, the personnel department, your peers – if they think it's a fair picture of what you're meant to be doing. It can lead to some extremely enlightening discussions! If you do have job descriptions in your organization, have a look at those for your boss and your subordinates, too, as they will give you an idea of what they should be doing and, perhaps even more important, what they should not be doing. A young manager I know asked her boss for a copy of his job description and received a very dusty response. 'Certainly not, it's none of your business,' he said. No wonder she was confused about the scope of her duties and responsibilities!

As you begin to form a picture of the activities that make up your job, list them under, say, ten headings, which may look something like:

1 reading and dealing with correspondence
2 counselling, training, 'personnel' matters

3 meetings (staff, suppliers, clients, etc.)
4 unscheduled meetings
5 trouble-shooting
6 planning
7 making and receiving telephone calls
8 reading
9 writing reports
10 travelling

You should, of course, change these to suit your particular situation. Calculate roughly how much time you ought to be spending on each of these activities, bearing in mind what the objectives of your job are. For instance, if you are in a service role, one of your main duties may be to deal with phone enquiries so, when you come to analysing your time log to see where time could be saved, you should not be considering cutting down the number of calls you deal with, but rather the way you deal with them. If you are self-employed, working as a sole trader or independent person, you can still do this exercise. Your list of activities might be something like:

1 writing proposals and reports
2 meetings (clients, suppliers, etc.)
3 marketing
4 accounts
5 travelling
6 working on assignments
7 networking
8 preparation and planning
9 reading and dealing with correspondence
10 general office, admin and 'housekeeping' matters

Now look closely at your time log and work out how much time you are spending on each activity corresponding to the list you compiled when analysing your job. Compare that with what you think you should be doing, and the discrepancy between the two lists will be the starting point for you to do something about changing your work pattern.

The next four charts may be used to carry out this exercise.

You should then carry the analysis a step further. (See pages 35 to 41.)

TIME LOG ANALYSIS

Stage 1

To identify your work tasks, list your actual job activities (continue the lists according to the number of tasks you do):

1

2

3

4

5

6

7

8

9

10

11

12

Stage 2

Taking those same activities, list them in order of importance as you see them in relation to your job – the most important item coming first:

1

2

3

4

5

6

7

8

9

10

11

12

Stage 3

To establish the areas of potential change in your use of time:

A how many hours per week do you spend on each of the items
   listed in stage 2?

B how much time should be spent on these tasks?

C what is the time difference between A and B?

Actual time spent (**A**)	Desired time spent (**B**)	Discrepancy between A & B (**C**)
1		
2		
3		
4		
5		
6		
7		
8		
9		
10		
11		
12		

Stage 4

To begin to make changes in your work pattern, list the items from stage 3C in which there are significant discrepancies:

1

2

3

4

5

6

These are the things you want to begin changing.

Look at your time log sheets and analyse the activities under various headings.

Outcome

- How successful were the various activities?

- Which activities did you fail to complete satisfactorily?

Type of work

Divide the activities into three categories:

1 Things you MUST do

2 Things you SHOULD do

3 Things you would LIKE to do

Allocate a percentage of your time to each of these categories according to their importance, for example:

1 75 per cent

2 20 per cent

3 5 per cent

Referring back to your time log sheets, how much time are you actually spending on these activities?

Often we concentrate on the things we are able to do easily, or the things we like doing, at the expense of those we find difficult. These difficult tasks may well be the most vital ones, those which constitute the 'What am I here for?' part of your job.

You could look at the proportion of time you spend on:

1 *Managerial work*
   e.g., planning, organizing, motivating

35

2 *Professional skills*
   e.g., using your specialist professional skills

As a manager, you will find that one of the greatest temptations is to slip back into exercising your old professional skills, such as accounting, engineering, sales, instead of developing your new managerial skills. Of course you will need to use these old skills from time to time but you need to judge how much is appropriate. You should be absolutely honest with yourself as to how much you are avoiding the difficulties and unknown problems of the new work, preferring the security and comfort of the old skills. Self-employed people find this difficult, too, particularly when they have to develop and use unfamiliar skills, such as marketing or basic office work. In these situations, there is rarely anyone around to bail you out if you get into a mess. However, if you have done your homework thoroughly before becoming self-employed, you may have been able to do some preliminary work on these areas and will be able to get by until you become more skilled at juggling all the activities you need to develop.

Where does the work come from?

1 Boss

   • is he delegating enough?

2 Subordinates

   • are they too dependent on you?

3 Yourself

   • are you setting yourself enough work?

4 Elsewhere

   • from where?
   • how important?

Delegation

When you look at the tasks you are undertaking, ask yourself:

- could this have been delegated?

When you have analysed the way you actually do spend your time, you have to begin thinking about the changes you have to bring about to make your use of time more effective.

1 What things are you doing now that you should not be doing in the first place?

2 What things should you be doing more of?

3 What things are you spending too much time on?

4 What things should you be delegating?

It is useful to repeat the time log exercise occasionally, say every six months, to check on your progress, to see if you have changed your work pattern and if you are spending more time on planning and strategy. It is so easy to slip back into bad habits that it is a good idea to remind yourself every so often of what you said you would try to change and improve.

You may be able to identify several ways in which you can begin changing. For example, you will be able to initiate some small changes immediately, on your own, but you may have to discuss others with your boss and/or the people you work with. You should, therefore, look at the things you want to change and decide whether you can change them alone, change them in discussion with others, or perhaps not be able to change them right now, but sometime in the future.

If you identify two or three areas which you think you can tackle now on your own, plan how you will make those

37

changes, try them out and then evaluate the results. Don't try to do too many all at once – there is nothing more dispiriting than starting something full of enthusiasm and coming across hurdles and objections at every turn. Most changes have to be brought in slowly and gently, so that everyone concerned knows what is going on and why. That is why I suggest that you start with something that you can change on your own, something not too startling to begin with, and then, as you build up confidence that the world will not fall apart if you introduce change, aim for something larger, involving more people, and then other people will want to know how you have managed to organize yourself so well.

The working day

When you have completed your time log and feel you have a better idea of how you are spending your time than you did before, you will need to use that information to manage your time more creatively and productively. Look at the following questions in the light of your analysis, either on your own or with someone else who will give you an honest opinion of where you are seen to be wasting time.

1 From my time log, what appears to be my major problem?

2 On whom or what am I spending too little time?

3 On whom or what am I spending too much time?

4 Which activities could have been done by another person?

5 Does 'personal development' appear anywhere in my list?

6 Does 'development of my staff' appear anywhere in my list?

39

7 Do I know which part of the day is my best time for creative thinking?

8 Can I cut down on travelling time?

9 Do I really need to attend all the meetings I go to?

10 Do I always know why I am going to a meeting?

11 Is my office/work space arranged in the way which is most conducive to effective working?

12 Do I spend most of my time reacting to other people's demands?

13 How much time do I spend initiating work?

14 How much time is spent firefighting?

15 How much time do I spend with my boss?

16 How much time do I spend with my secretary and other support staff?

17 Do I ever ask for other people's help or advice on how to improve my use of time?

18 Do I answer all my telephone calls myself?

19 Do I ever finish a task in one go?

20 What is the longest period of time I have given to one activity, without interruption, during the time log exercise?

Managers and their jobs

There has been quite a lot of research done into the nature of managerial work and if you are interested in delving deeper into this aspect of your job you should look at *The Nature of Managerial Work* by Henry Mintzberg (Harper and Row, New York), *Managers and Their Jobs* by Rosemary Stewart (Macmillan, London) and *The Effective Executive* by Peter Drucker (Heinemann and Pan, London).

The most comprehensive study of British managers and the way they spend their time was that carried out by Rosemary Stewart in *Managers and Their Jobs* and, as far as I am aware, there has not been a similar study done by

41

anyone else since. There are, however, increasing numbers of studies, articles and books on the subject of competencies and these include those for managerial jobs. The primary aim of Rosemary Stewart's research was to develop a classification of managers' work which would be useful in the selection of managers because it would help to highlight characteristics of the job not usually included in job descriptions. It would also show if the job to be filled was of a different type from the person's previous job. The emphasis would be on the interpersonal relationships characterizing the job.

The three main divisions within the classification were:

1 *Internal* where there is little or no contact with people outside the organization

2 *Internal/External* where jobs are primarily concerned with relationships within the organization but which have more external contacts

3 *External* where dealing with people outside the organization is a major characteristic of the job

If we look at the internal category, the various management roles may be subdivided as shown below:

1 Hub jobs where relationships are spread fairly evenly among peers, seniors and subordinates

2 Peer-dependent jobs where the manager's main contacts are with colleagues of the same level, and where the emphasis is on persuasion rather than authority for the successful completion of objectives

3 Man-management jobs where most of the contacts are with subordinates

4 Solo jobs where there are few contacts and where the manager concerned has to work to regular time deadlines with a low level of uncertainty

Similar types of work are to be found in other categories, but with differing emphases.

From her studies, Rosemary Stewart showed that the very nature of managers' jobs posed certain dangers to efficiency.

Superficiality
Since the manager's work is so fragmented and he spends much of his time responding to stimuli provided by other people, there is a danger that he will not distinguish sufficiently between the work that is relatively unimportant and that which requires greater thought.

Responding rather than initiating
A manager may become like a puppet with other people pulling the strings, rather than someone who consciously determines the priorities of his work.

Grasshoppering
Since so much of the manager's work is episodic, he may find it hard to settle to any task that requires concentrated attention and, instead, be diverted to deal with something different even though it may be unimportant.

Attractions of being busy
Busyness may be at the expense of thinking about objectives and priorities.

Too busy to listen
A manager may think he is readily available to his staff but does he take the time to listen to what they say?

Lack of communication
The more senior the manager, the greater the danger that he may not communicate to his subordinates the informal information that he has obtained from his diverse contacts.

43

Rosemary Stewart puts forward the following ideas to counteract the above dangers:

1 The manager should plan to pass on to his staff the information that only he receives through his wider contacts and from being in a position to see a broader picture of the organization.

2 The manager can deal with the dangers of superficiality by distinguishing those issues that can be delegated or dealt with quickly from those that need greater concentration and depth of understanding.

3 Once a manager has made commitments, for example, sitting on a committee, he has mortgaged some of his time. Therefore, one of his important decisions is about what commitments he is undertaking.

4 The manager should make the most of the opportunities provided by the things he must do. For example, during an inspection tour, one manager may only be monitoring what is happening, while another manager may also be actively looking for possible improvements in the way things are done.

5 The manager should be seeing broadly while looking narrowly. There is a danger that concern for detail may obscure the broad issues.

6 The manager should examine how he works. There is a danger that he is spending too much time on the things that he enjoys, or is familiar with, and too little time on other things. Most managers benefit from asking themselves what they ought to be doing and then keeping a record of what they are actually doing. They are usually surprised at the difference between the two.

Other common failings of managers were seen to be:

Blaming the individual when it is the situation
It is easier to blame the individual than to consider whether there are special strains and stresses in the job and in the organization of work.

Stressing people's weaknesses rather than their strengths
Drucker's advice: 'There is no such thing as a "good man". Good for what? is the question.'

Being cut off the higher you go in the hierarchy
Some loneliness is inevitable, particularly in the top job, but some dangers can be avoided by trying to keep in touch with what people are thinking and feeling. Beware the carefully edited information.

Moral cowardice
Avoiding painful decisions, especially when they involve others.

The research that has been carried out into the nature of managerial work is useful for managers who want to be clear in their own minds what they should be doing. When they have discovered this it becomes easier to decide which tasks are to be done by them, which are to be delegated, and which should not be accepted in the first place.

When the work side of your life has become clearer, then you can begin to look more broadly at how you cope with the demands on your time by the organization and by other outside influences.

What do I want?

When there seems to be too much to do at work, it is difficult to see how other activities can fit in. Most managers work to earn the money to maintain a comfortable standard of living, and to be fulfilled by their jobs. However, if the job ceases to be satisfying or challenging in a constructive way, and becomes a burden because of the lack of time to do anything properly, and if this means that there is less chance to enjoy the opportunities that present themselves to those who now have discretionary spending power, the two main motivators are not being met.

Recently on time management courses, I have been asking the managers participating to spend some time answering the question 'What do I want?' so that they may begin to think of where work fits into their whole lives, and about its relative importance to home and leisure. Often the managers have not looked at this question except in times of crisis and for some people it is quite a painful exercise. The results have been fascinating, sometimes predictable but often surprising, revealing hidden ambitions and aspirations. Frequently the chance to express these wishes has come as a great relief, and the managers have welcomed the opportunity to look in depth at the way their lives are going and how they are going to influence that direction if it is not altogether satisfactory at the moment.

When a manager has expressed his need to spend more time with his young family in the evenings, or his intention to become a better tennis player, or his wish to devote more time to some voluntary activity, he begins to see that he must cut down on overtime where possible and then the advantages of organizing the working day more effectively become clearer. We all have an idea in the back of our minds that we aren't getting the most out of the day and that we should not be spending so much time at work, but it is useful to be more definite about what we want and thus eliminate the fuzzy edges. Of course, facing up to your life can be a chastening or saddening experience but it should also help you to plan ahead in terms of where work fits into your whole life. Naturally, there will be many situations where a manager may not want to go home at the end of a 'normal' working day but it is useful to understand what is driving you on to work extra hours, or what is making you eke out your day regardless of the quantity of work to be tackled. As with many of the exercises, it is worth looking at 'What do I want?' from time to time, as people's priorities change with their circumstances. For example, a young man with no family ties may identify different ambitions today from five years hence when he has to help support a partner, child and mortgage.

If you now feel clearer about how much time you think you should be spending at work, you can go on to look at how best to organize that time, to accomplish everything that needs to be done without having to do overtime every night and without having to take work home on a regular basis.

(One way of committing 'What do I want?' to paper is to use the brainstorming technique outlined on pages 90–93).

Setting priorities

When you know there are a certain number of things to do during the day or the coming week, it is useful to give each task a priority in relation to the others.

Write a list of all the jobs you have to get done, not just the immediate problems of today, but all the long-term objectives and tasks. They need not be in any particular order – just brainstorm and write down everything that comes into your mind. That alone will probably throw you into a panic and make you want to start work immediately, since you know you don't have time to do it all, but take a deep breath and go on to the next step.

The list of tasks that you have is doubtless a mixture of small and large items, urgent and not-so-urgent, boring and exciting, short-term and long-term. Your first job is to

47

identify which of these are the *active* tasks and which are the *reactive* tasks.

Active   those tasks you must do to achieve the objectives of your job. These are the tasks that answer the question: 'WHAT AM I HERE FOR?'

Reactive   those tasks which are the routine bits and pieces which turn up every day and have to be dealt with to keep things ticking over. You will never get any praise or thanks for completing these jobs so you should aim to get them done and out of the way as quickly as possible.

You will already recognize that most managers seem to spend their available time on the reactive tasks – just coping with the day-to-day jobs – and spend very little time on the active tasks. Many self-employed people spend a great deal of time working on their assignments and not enough on the 'maintenance' of their business, most of which includes routine, everyday tasks. This is why so many small businesses fail – their inability or unwillingness to monitor all aspects of the business leads to a poor cash flow, not enough new jobs, a nervous breakdown, and so on.

When you have put all your activities under one of the above two categories, remembering that you only give active status to those jobs which help you to build the business and achieve the objectives of the organization, you can begin to schedule your work into the time you have available.

It is necessary to know two things about a task before you can give it a priority:

1   How long do you need to spend on the task?
    (That is determined by how *important* that task is.)

2   How soon do you have to complete the task?
    (That is determined by how *urgent* the task is.)

Importance and urgency are not the same thing. An urgent task is not necessarily important. It may be urgent but trivial, for example, the allocation of locker space in the new cloakrooms, so you should deal with this sort of task straightaway – don't put it off and don't spend all morning on it. That way you'll leave yourself plenty of time for the important tasks.

Reactive tasks are often not important, whereas the active tasks are nearly always important. If something is important *and* urgent, then it must be given high priority.

It is essential to give important, active tasks enough time so that the work is completed within the deadline. You can then slot reactive tasks into your schedule or when unexpected gaps appear in the timetable – for example, when a meeting is postponed for half an hour.

I must admit that 'urgent' is a word that I try not to use because I'm not sure what it means any more. Except in cases of life and death, 'urgent' has become an overused word which encourages people to react without thinking. It's rather like 'asap'. I find it more helpful to ascertain what the real timetable for the work is, a date and time when it needs to be ready and I can then schedule my own work more accurately. Sometimes, 'urgent' tasks disappear or the deadline passes without dire results. For example, if a memo marked 'urgent' is put in your pigeonhole and you're suddenly away sick for a few days, what happens? Either someone else deals with it or it waits until you get back and are able to do what is necessary.

Planning ahead

Many people have a fear of planning ahead, of thinking far enough into the future to know how to organize the next few weeks or months. I think this is often because they believe that to have specific events written down will restrict them in some way, that they will become bogged down in routine and therefore less flexible. However, I think it is really because they cannot organize themselves enough to know what is going on in the near future, or that in some cases they would rather not know what is going to happen.

The organized manager will be aware of future events such as the annual conference, the quarterly management meeting, the monthly departmental get-together, the weekly staff meeting, the half-yearly budget, and he will put them in his diary and on his yearly planner as soon as possible.

If these events are clearly recorded somewhere, it is easier to do any necessary preparatory work for them in good time rather than panic at the last minute because, for some strange reason, you had forgotten that the monthly report was due again at the end of this month! I always feel that's a bit like the amazement with which the British greet the winter every year: 'Good heavens, it's snowing – what a surprise!'

There are several ways in which you can plan ahead. I am not going to say you should use any particular one because each of you will have your own preferences. This is one reason I am hesitant to recommend categorically any of the systems currently on the market – if they suit you, that's fine, but if they don't, you may be able to use something else.

The humble diary can be one of your most useful management tools. As it stands, the ordinary desk diary ordered for you by your company may not look very promising as a planning aid but, with a little modification and imagination, it can become what my husband calls his 'life support system'.

If you take a typical diary, such as the one shown in Figure 3, it doesn't tempt you to use it as more than an historical record of meetings and perhaps expenses. However, if you spend just a few minutes modifying it at the beginning of the year, you could have something that looks like Figure 4 which is of much more use.

As I said, the above idea is just one way of using your diary and, with a little thought, you can probably think of other ways to adapt your present diary. One manager I know has adopted an unusual system for marking his diary to show that, for example, he should begin to prepare for an important conference in three weeks' time. He marks the diary pages with the signs for leaving a motorway three, two and one week away from the event. This flags up the impending work to be done and doesn't leave him in the position of turning the page one Sunday evening and realizing he has only a few days left to prepare.

At the beginning of each day, it is worth putting aside some time, say fifteen minutes, to jot down the tasks that have to be tackled. They should then be looked at in terms of being active or reactive, important or urgent, to be done by you or delegated, and so on. You can then assign priorities to each activity and, where possible, allocate time to them. Some people prefer to do this at the end of the previous day. Neither way is better than the other, just a matter of preference.

There is a great feeling of satisfaction in crossing off each activity from the list as you complete it. Even if it is only one task, you feel as if you have achieved something today. Anything that is not completed today can be transferred to tomorrow and its relative importance or urgency assessed in relation to the new activities that present themselves then.

It is possible to enter some activities into the daily plan with a degree of certainty. Some managers I have worked with have made a conscious effort to put aside the first half hour of the day to go on a 'walkabout' round the department, just so that they keep abreast of what is going on, from a work point of view as well as the social. At first, their staff wondered what was going on, but now they see it as an opportunity to keep them up to date with problems and progress on a regular footing, without having to pin them

Figure 3

1993 August		1993 August	
Monday 5 Week 32 0930 Staff meeting Lunch - Bill		**Thursday 8** 10.00 Campaign presentation	
Tuesday 6 2.00 Appraisal-Mary 4.00 Graphics people		**Friday 9** Lunch - Gordon and Kathy 3.15 Fred's leaving	
Wednesday 7 9.00 Sales managers 2.30 Meeting with Mr. Beauchamp		**Saturday 10**	
		Sunday 11	

Figure 4

1993 August

Monday 5
Week 32

0900 ↔	Mail	
0930	Staff meeting - my office	
1030 ↔ ↔	Lunch - Bill - canteen	
1230		
1330	Dictation + check Thursday with Mary	
1430 ↔		
1700	OPEN DOOR	

TO DO
Presentation

Graphics costings

Staff meeting minutes

Sales training programmes

Tuesday 6

0900 ↔	Mail	
0930 ↔		
1050		
1150 ↔		
1230	Lunch	
1330	Mary's appraisal	
1400 ↔		
1500		
1600	Graphics - room 314 - material for Thursday	

Appraisal preparation

Staff meeting minutes

Check progress on MacDonald project

Wednesday 7

0900 ↔	Sales managers	
1030	No 2 Conference room	
1100	Mail and dictation	
1230	Lunch	
1300		
1430	Mr Beauchamp - his office - final arrangements for Thursday	

Check:
Mongeress happy about Thursday

Write:
Helman and Co
Mitchell Bros
Wayne Dixon

1993 August

Thursday 8

1000 ↔	Campaign presentation	
1200	No 1 Conference room	
1230	Lunch - director's dining room	
1430	Mail and messages	
1500	Review of presentation	

TO DO:

Check:
a/v equipment
Coffee and lunch

Follow up
thank
Mrs Haines

Friday 9

0830 ↔	Mail and dictation	
0930 ↔↔	OPEN DOOR	
1200 ↔	Lunch with Gordon and Kathy at	
1250		
1330 ↔	Bread + Pullet	
1400	Phone and messages	
1515	Fred's leaving tea - post room	

Book lunch at Bread and Pullet

write to:
solicitors
Mrs Wilson
Wayne Dixon

Think about additional staff

Buy present for John Baxter

Saturday 10

0930 swimming with kids

2000 Dinner at Butlers

For next week:
agenda for departmental meeting

Sunday 11

1000 Tennis

Afternoon - gardening

ask new client about campaign

Talk to Peters about house style

down to a specific meeting during the day. If they do need to see them, they mention it at the beginning of the day and are told when the managers are free. As these managers have also established times when they are free every week, their staff know when they are not available (except for real emergencies) and everyone seems to like knowing exactly what is going on.

If you don't like using a traditional diary, you might like to design your own daily plan. An example is given opposite. It is drawn onto a punched, A4 sheet and photocopied as needed. You will see that everything is recorded, including personal and social events as I think it is almost impossible to divorce the various parts of your life from one another.

You might prefer to make the sheet smaller, say A5, as it would be more portable that way, but it is very much a personal choice.

In this example, I have put aside a period in the early afternoon for making telephone calls. This will not suit everybody, and indeed it may not be feasible, but it is just a suggestion as to one of the ways in which you can begin to organize your days. If someone is keeping messages for you, or if the answering machine is recording them, deal with as many as you can in one session. The practical reason for choosing the early afternoon used to be that it was cheaper to use the phone then than during the morning.

I've deliberately set aside time for lunch each day. I think it is vital to take a definite break in the middle of the day and I don't really like too many working lunches. I'm sure the body likes to concentrate on either digesting food which is eaten in relaxed surroundings or coping with the demands of important company matters, but not both together!

I'm not against lunch altogether, believe me, but I think that many managers eat too much of the wrong things at this time of day. This is particularly relevant if you are the kind of person who won't or can't take any physical exercise. If you

Figure 5

Daily Plan	Date 2 September 1993
Fixed appointments	**TASKS** **Priority**
0800	- Look at pension fund B proposals
0900 Check diary with Penny	
	- snagging on A Hillview*
1000 Ron: final drawing for feasibility study	
	- Revisions to Winter bourne A drawings
1100 Final edit of feasibility study	
1200 ⎧	
⎨ LUNCH	
1300 ⎩	**SPEAK/WRITE TO:**
1400 Messages/telephone calls	- QS ②
* Brief Chas on snagging	- Colin ①
1500	- Wilson & Ptnrs ③
1600	
1700	**REMEMBER!**
1800	- rail tickets (Chelmsford)
1900	- Colin's present
2000 Dinner: Gilberts	

NOTES

Petrol £20 Access

don't keep yourself fit because you don't have the time to do anything but work and sleep, that is all the more reason to watch what and how you eat. If it is possible to go for a short walk during the lunch break, just to get away from the working environment, I'm sure that is also beneficial.

There are all kinds of wall charts and planners available to deal with events such as training courses, staff holidays, sales campaigns, and you will need to look at them to see which is most appropriate for you. In some companies, there are rules which state that nothing shall be pinned up on the walls or, in the case of open-plan offices, on the sides of the filing cabinets. This means that most of the large size charts are not possible, but there are some on the market which are the size of blotters and can therefore sit on your desk.

It should be a rule in your office that you deal with every piece of paper that drops on your desk within a few hours of its arrival. Some people say that a piece of paper should cross your desk only once. This may mean just indicating whether it is for you to deal with, or whether you will delegate it, and giving it an A, B or C priority. It may need filing, either in a cabinet or the time-honoured way, in the w.p.b.! For those papers that do not have to be dealt with immediately, but are important, one way of keeping them in sight, but not cluttering up the desk, is in a 'bring forward' file. There are several of these on the market, some just divided into alphabetical sections but others showing days of the week, months, quarters as well. It is up to you to decide which is the most appropriate for you. Two examples are shown in Figure 6. Advances in IT mean that there are now many ways of using your computer to jog your memory, or perhaps you have one of the 'pocket' systems. While many people really enjoy playing with this advanced technology, others are not so enthralled by it, which is why I've still included the more traditional methods.

The important thing to remember about all these aids is

Figure 6

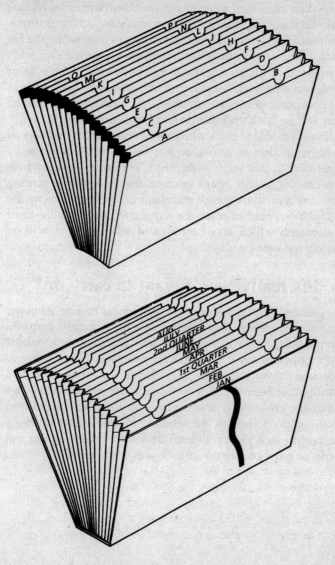

that they must be kept up to date or they become a waste of time. You may not want to get involved with this routine task but there are others who may well enjoy it, for example, your secretary. It is vital that she knows exactly what you are doing, where you are going, who you are seeing and why.

If you don't have a secretary, then leave a note on your desk, leave your diary open, put a message on the door or in the computer network – anything to let people know when you will be back and able to deal with their call.

If you are able to put a whiteboard or something similar on your wall, this is a useful way of showing your daily timetable. If, in a large office, there is a central point where you can put a large board or chart, this is useful for writing down where the various members of the department are today. You could also have a supplementary, smaller chart underneath which gives an idea of where people will be during the coming days.

Is this really how I want to carry on?

As you read the description of the young manager below, you may recognize your own hectic life but now that you have read through this chapter, you will be able to take a more objective view of what is happening.

If you know someone like Martin, you may now feel confident enough to offer him some advice so that he can avoid the crisis he is undoubtedly heading for. Be careful how you do it, though. Remember how difficult it has been for you to face your problems and admit that you are the cause of most of them, just as it was for Martin.

STUDY 4

Martin Reed was a young computer software writer who had recently been promoted to a management post. He had always been popular with the other people in the department and was known as someone who would always join in any fun that was going on. He could also be relied on to help out if the work was running a bit behind schedule and it was assumed that this would still be the case, even if he had become a manager.

He always lived life to the full and when his first child was born the whole section had celebrated in great style.

About six weeks after his promotion, people began to remark that Martin was looking a bit haggard, but put it down to sleepless nights with the baby. However, they still assumed that he would be going to a colleague's stag night even though he had also promised to play rugby the next day. He was also reminded that he had volunteered to help out on a rush project that would mean two or three hours' overtime each evening for a couple of weeks.

One of his colleagues remarked how kind it had been of Martin to stand in for him at a progress meeting, especially as he had also had to write a report for the monthly review, but he had been assured that Martin didn't mind missing his lunch at all — he had snatched a couple of sandwiches while he read his post and he had soon caught up.

His boss commented one day that he had heard Martin say he and his wife were hoping to start evening classes in navigation soon. The boss was a bit concerned as to how he was going to fit that in, since Martin had agreed to write a technical procedures manual for the department by Easter.

Martin was wondering how he was going to break the news to his parents that he wouldn't be able to attend their ruby wedding anniversary in the summer. He just had to hope that they would understand how important it was for him to attend the sales trip to Scotland because the director was relying on him to make a good impression.

CHAPTER 2

How to organize yourself

Now that you know the reasons for your lack of time to think and plan ahead, you can begin to introduce ways of changing your work pattern and improving the use of time.

You cannot organize other people until you have learned to organize yourself, and this chapter will offer practical ways of managing the timewasters. As they stand, some of these suggestions may not be immediately relevant to your own situation, but with a little imagination most of them can be modified.

Some of them mean that you may have to take a deep breath or even a certain amount of risk before you can implement them. People normally don't like to rock the boat or have the boat rocked for them and you will come up against some resistance to new ideas.

Other remedies will mean some plain, old-fashioned graft to get them into operation. For instance, there is no short cut to learning how to read more quickly and effectively, so you will have to keep the advantages of this new skill to the forefront of your mind if you are to remain motivated.

Open door and closed door

It has long been a boast of managers who want to be thought of as approachable, 'Oh, my office door is always open.' We all know that there are some people who you wouldn't go near, whether or not the door was permanently open, and those who you don't think twice about disturbing even if the door is firmly closed. What you want to achieve is the happy situation where a closed door indicates that you are not, on any account, to be disturbed because you are doing something which requires concentration and quiet. On the other hand, you want people to know that, if your door is open, you will be willing to see them and, indeed, that is the main purpose for making yourself obviously accessible.

One of the benefits of planning your time more effectively is that you should have a clearer idea of when you need to be shut away and when you can be available for people to call in with problems or for a chat. If you leave, say, a couple of afternoons a week free to deal with minor tasks which can easily be put aside if someone needs to see you, that means the rest of the time can be devoted to the positive activities which form the basis of your work. If people get used to the notion that you are not generally available, except at stated times, they will soon get into the habit of making specific appointments or remembering to see you during your 'open door' period.

When you have identified the tasks that are important, those vital to the success of the business, you have to put aside the time to deal with them, but sometimes this is not as difficult as finding a suitable place to do that work. This is particularly true if you work in an open-plan space or share an office with someone else. If you can't be sure that you will remain undisturbed for a reasonable amount of time, you may have to use a meeting room, or a spare office, or maybe work at home to ensure that you complete the task. This latter option is not always feasible, especially if you have young children who might be so excited by having you at home that you would not be allowed to work in peace! If a conference room is available, you might be able to book it in the normal way for a couple of hours, and we all know that two hours' clear run at a job is worth almost a whole day in a busy office.

If you need to work with your team for a day or two, but realize that the chances of being able to do that in the office are low, you could hire a room at a local hotel or conference centre. I know of several companies who are beginning to see this as a perfectly legitimate expense because the results gained in a short time of uninterrupted discussion far outweigh the financial outlay.

One manager's solution to the problem of not being allowed to work undisturbed in an open-plan office struck me as helpful and I've passed it on successfully to many others. She puts up a red flag on her desk to indicate that she is not to be bothered. The flag is put away when she's finished that piece of work. 'The flag means I'm not there even if you can see me,' she told me. 'If it's not there, I'm available to talk. I have to be scrupulously honest in the way I use this method so that people know I really mean it when the flag's flying.' Other managers who have adopted this idea use teddy bears or other soft toys, move a potted plant to a specific spot on the desk or they put a striking display on their computer screen. This may sound somewhat bizarre, but surely it's worth it if you can polish off that report or deal with that difficult sales forecast?

The telephone

One of the most common causes of frustration and distress among managers is the continuous demands of the telephone on their time. With the introduction of new technology it is becoming easier to divert calls or redial, but these techniques are still not used universally.

One of the main aspects of your job may be to deal with telephone queries, so you obviously have to accept that you must deal with calls, even if they interrupt other work. If, however, you don't see telephone conversations as the major task in achieving the objectives of your organization, you need to reduce the number of unnecessary calls you receive during the working day.

If you have a secretary, or other subordinates, you can route calls through them. Indeed, it is the responsibility of a secretary to shield her boss from unnecessary calls which will waste his time. It is her duty to recognize those callers to whom you will wish to speak, and to know how to handle the others tactfully. Very often she can deal with the call herself, answer any queries or provide the information, but if she can't, she must take a message and assure the caller that you will ring back at a certain time. If she can get an idea of what the caller wants, she can forewarn her boss so that he may get together any information he needs before he rings back.

When you need some undisturbed time, it may be possible to persuade one of your colleagues to take your calls for, say, a couple of hours and promise to do the same for him next time he is in the same position. Advise the switchboard to put all your calls through to your colleague, who then just takes a name, number and perhaps a short message, promising that you will return the call before the end of the day. You should then be able to use that extra time to great effect. It is essential, in such a case, that you do call back when you say you will as people will be much more inclined to leave a message with someone else in future.

In an open-plan office where several of you are receiving calls on the same line, you could come to an agreement whereby one person takes all the calls for a set time and someone else takes over later. As long as the caller knows that he will be rung back within, say, half an hour, he will usually be quite content. There are not many matters that can't wait for thirty minutes.

If you are a one-man band, or regularly in the office on your own for prolonged periods, you might invest in an answering machine. As long as you keep to your word that you will call back within an hour, most people will be quite happy to leave their names and numbers.

There are times when a telephone should not be allowed to interrupt proceedings. During a meeting, for example, or in an interview, it is too disruptive and, in the case of an interview, downright rude. You may just have to take the receiver off the hook, but it is best to conduct meetings and interviews in a room without a phone.

When you are giving dictation to your secretary and the phone rings, you should let her take the call. She can then say that you are busy for a few minutes and will call back shortly. That way, the disruption is minimal and you will resist the temptation to deal with the call, leaving the secretary sitting twiddling her thumbs.

When people are taking telephone messages, make sure that they are getting sufficient information and presenting it in an acceptable form. Some people seem to find this difficult but let them know exactly what you want from them and they should soon get the idea.

The telephone has many advantages. For example, it can save you walking or driving to see someone about a relatively trivial matter. You can clear up a query quickly and avoid the socializing that a face-to-face encounter usually entails. It is only when you are continually interrupted in the middle of periods of concentration, and when some of the calls could be dealt with by someone else, that it becomes a nuisance. If you learn to control it, either with the help of other people or the new technology, it can be an ally, rather than an enemy.

Unscheduled interruptions

Most people who have completed a time log agree that they were most concerned about the number of unscheduled interruptions they allowed to happen during a day. They all knew that there were people stopping by for a quick chat and that they answered the telephone a great many times during the day but, until they had seen it written down, they had not realized how disruptive those interruptions had been.

Typical examples include the people who come into the office and demand your attention, regardless of whether you are giving dictation or having a conversation with somebody else.

Some people seem to be incapable of reading the signs that you are busy, do not have the time or inclination to stop to discuss the weather or yesterday's upset in the canteen and it is difficult to know what to do, short of being rude. You may have to be kind, but firm, and interrupt the visitor, saying 'John, I'm sorry but I really can't stop and chat now. If you'd like to call back at four o'clock, I'll have a couple of minutes to talk to you then. OK?' If John really has something worth saying, he'll come back at four, but if he was just at a loose end, he probably won't bother to return. He may not even remember what he was going to say to you anyway!

Similarly, you probably answer all the phone calls that are put through to you and deal with them immediately 'just to get that out of the way'.

Another problem is the sudden meeting that is called at a few minutes' notice. You're not really sure what it's about and the secretary who called you doesn't know either – she's just been told by her boss to get hold of you.

These are interruptions which are timewasters. There are many others which are not – those which are part of your job – and so it is not possible to say that all unscheduled interruptions should be refused.

However, if an interruption is not helping you to achieve the objectives of your job, if it is wasting your time, then you should try to find ways of minimizing the negative consequences or ensure that it doesn't happen again.

The open-door policy is one which most managers try to follow, believing that they should always be seen to be available to anyone who wants to see them. This is clearly counterproductive and it is possible to arrange your week in such a way that, while you can set aside specific times to deal with reactive tasks and important interruptions, there is a system whereby you are not constantly disturbed by unimportant phone calls or casual visitors.

There are occasions when it is necessary to close the door and get on with a task without fear of interruption. If you do this only when it is absolutely necessary, potential intruders will soon get to know that if the door is closed, it is closed for a good reason. In such cases, the visitor could make an appointment with your secretary or leave a message for you to call back when you are free. (Incidentally, next time you go into a colleague's office, ask yourself if you really need to see him or if you are just doing to him what so annoys you when done by somebody else!)

All this assumes that you have a door to open or close! In open-plan offices, it is not possible to hide away behind a closed door and you will then have to devise some way of indicating that you are not to be disturbed (see p. 63). If there is no secretary nearby to protect you, perhaps you could put a notice on the front of your desk that indicates when you will be free from the work that is presently occupying you.

Socializing is all part of office life but, taken to extremes, it can be very disruptive and most people find it quite hard to deal with. You don't want to be seen to be unfriendly, but you know you have to end this conversation soon. One way to deal with this is to conduct the conversation standing up. The caller then has less opportunity to sit down, make himself comfy and settle himself in for a long chat. Certainly, if you need to get a particular job done quickly, you must resist the temptation to offer a cup of coffee or any other friendly, sociable indication that you are free to talk.

If you know somebody wants to speak to you, you may find it best to go to his office or desk where you have more control over how long the encounter lasts. It is much easier for you to end the conversation by leaving the office.

A secretary can play a vital part in blocking interruptions. She should make appointments for you, perhaps only tentative ones if there is any doubt about your availability, but if she has the authority to fix times for you, that will save time. You could try to put aside specific times for people to come and see you which would make the task even easier for your secretary.

You will usually have a good idea of how long a visit should last and if you tell the caller at the beginning how much time is available, then you both know how long you have to talk. You could also prime your secretary so that she can let you know when the prescribed time is coming to an end.

We saw earlier how a secretary can also handle a good proportion of your telephone calls. You could help here by telling callers that, in future, they should ask for her as she will have the necessary information or will know where to get it. In this way, they will get used to asking the secretary direct. The same applies to anyone working with or for you. Just because you are the boss, it does not necessarily mean you are the best person to deal with a query. The person who is dealing with the matter all the time is the obvious one to speak to.

Many offices now have call-forward facilities on their telephone systems and this is invaluable if you don't want to be disturbed. You should make it clear beforehand if you don't want to be interrupted under any circumstances, or if there are some people who you will talk to.

You cannot refuse to see everybody or you would never know what was going on. You can, however, reduce the number of timewasting interruptions and this is invaluable if you need to have time to think.

Meetings

I shall be looking at two types of meeting in this section. The first is the formal, scheduled meeting and the second is the unscheduled meeting, when people are drawn together at very short notice in a less formal way.

Of the many definitions of the word 'meeting' in the *Oxford English Dictionary*, three in particular seem to apply to those generally frustrating gatherings which take up a great deal of the working week:

> The action of coming together from opposite or different directions into one place or into the presence of each other, of assembling for the transaction of business, etc.

> An encounter in arms; a fight, battle; a duel.

> An assembly of people for purpose of worship.

While the first definition is the one most of you will recognize, you would probably agree that there is an element of the other two in many of the meetings you attend!

Meetings generally imply a planned arrangement for people to get together to give or exchange information, or to solve a problem.

As you probably spend a lot of time in meetings of all kinds, let's look first at the basic question: 'Is this meeting really necessary?' All too often people meet regularly because they have been meeting every week at that time for the last year and it has become a habit. It may be that the original terms of reference for that particular group of people to come together are now obsolete and there is no real need for that meeting to be held on a regular basis. The terms of reference may have altered, in which case you need to change the people involved, the timing, the location.

Often meetings are held 'for the sake of good communications' but, if there is nothing to communicate, they are a waste of time.

Before you next call a meeting, consider the alternatives. Could the matter be dealt with by a letter, a memo, a phone call, or a simple conversation between you and one other person? Sometimes five minutes spent with six people separately is more effective and productive than a half-hour meeting with them all together.

The composition of a group meeting together is also very important. Often people attend a meeting only to find that they are directly concerned with just one item, or that one of their staff could have dealt with the matter equally well. There are often too many people at meetings, people who attend because 'they've always come along', or 'we can't risk offending him by not inviting him', or 'you never can tell, we might just need him'.

If there are too many people in a meeting, not everyone will have a chance to contribute and you have probably been to meetings where the wrong people have held court while those with relevant information or worthwhile opinions have not been able to have their say.

There are, of course, many positive sides to meetings. The coming together of a group of people may serve to confirm their existence as a team, and this may be very important, especially if they are working under pressure on a vital project.

In some cases, a meeting may be the only opportunity a group has to get together when the boss is actually seen as the leader of the team, rather than as the senior person to whom individuals report.

There are several things a chairperson must sort out before a meeting takes place if it is to run smoothly and effectively.

First, 'What is this meeting intended to achieve?' The objective may be to discuss a report, current progress on a project, a new policy or how to approach a potential new job. Whatever it is, it must be clear in the chairperson's mind before the agenda is sent out.

The agenda should not be just a list of the topics to be covered during a meeting. It should be properly drawn up to indicate whether an item is for information, for discussion or for decision, and it should give a brief description of the matter to be covered. For example, the heading 'Budget' is too brief and vague, whereas 'Budget: to discuss the client's proposal to reduce the money available for landscaping in favour of more sophisticated security systems' gives people the opportunity to devote some thought to the topic beforehand and form some views.

The order of items is important, especially when a decision on one topic will affect discussion of another. You may decide to put non-controversial items at the beginning and end of the agenda so that the meeting starts and finishes on a high note, but, equally, you must make sure that important subjects are discussed at a time when people are still feeling constructive and lively.

Most people would agree that a meeting should not go on for too long, and one of the ways of avoiding this is to allocate a time to each item and make sure that this is not exceeded. (In brainstorming sessions, it is not always possible to be as strict as this, but even here there is a limit to the time you can be genuinely creative and innovative.)

It is also a good idea to indicate the finishing time of a meeting on the agenda as well as the starting time.

'Any Other Business' on an agenda is an invitation to timewasting. This does not mean that the chairperson should not set aside time for extra items if something really urgent and unforeseen turns up but, generally speaking, the subjects should be known and prepared for beforehand.

It is very useful if background or supporting papers and documents are sent out with the agenda and not produced at the meeting. This not only saves time but it also helps people to think about the topic and formulate questions. These papers should not, however, be too long or people will not read them.

Any papers for a meeting should not be circulated too long before the meeting – people will only lose or forget them – but, on the other hand, adequate time should be given for reading supporting documents if appropriate.

The chairperson's task can sometimes be difficult, especially if the subject matter is sensitive or unpleasant, but a good chairperson can ensure that a meeting runs on time, covers the agenda in the prescribed time, and achieves the objectives laid down. He or she will also cope with any difficult group members, disagreements, red herrings and misunderstandings.

The chairperson must always be in control and should make sure that the group members understand what is to be achieved by discussing the issues and, if necessary, should suggest ways of tackling the subject, especially if it is long and complex. The chairperson must make sure that people with special knowledge of a subject are allowed to speak so that informed decisions may be made. Ideally, a chairperson should be neutral about topics being discussed but this is often not possible. When the chairperson has a useful contribution to make, she could relinquish the chair to someone else for the duration of that discussion and resume it later. That way, objectivity is maintained.

At the end of each item on the agenda, the chairperson should give a brief and clear summary of what has been decided and may even dictate the actual words to be used in the minutes to the person acting as secretary. This lessens the chances of mistakes being made or disagreements being brought up later by any of the people present. If an action is given to someone at the meeting, the chairperson should ensure that the delegate understands and accepts that action.

Minutes of a meeting should be sent out within a couple of days, especially if there are a number of actions to be carried out. If it is not possible to do this, then a summary could be made of the actions agreed and distributed immediately at the end of the meeting. A sheet similar to the one shown in Figure 7 could be used as a simple way of recording actions during a meeting, and then copied and distributed before everyone leaves.

The skills of chairing a meeting or taking minutes are useful and difficult to acquire without practice. I know of several organizations where, for small departmental meetings, the jobs of chairperson and minute-taker are rotated around the group so everyone has the chance to experience each role.

Could the next study be you? Facing yet another meeting do you get the feeling that they are beginning to run you, rather than the other way round? If you really need to hold the meeting or attend someone else's, think of ways to make it as brief and productive as possible.

Figure 7

Meeting: _____ Date: _____ Sheet .... of ....

Item	Action description	By whom	By when	Priority	Date completed

Chairman's Signature ....

STUDY 5

Derek Harrison had risen up through the ranks at a chemical works and at the age of forty-nine had become works manager. He was very pleased with the way things were working out generally, because he knew everybody and also how things were done in the company.

However, he did express a concern to a close colleague and friend one evening when they were having a drink in the local pub. He felt that most of his working day seemed to be made up of meetings, many of which went on too long, and he wasn't always sure why he was there. Because of his position, he was usually in the chair and that meant he also had to write the agendas and minutes. He said that it was a good thing that agendas were so simple and quick to put together because he could do them the day before and it didn't seem to matter if they weren't given out until the start of the meeting. Anyway, he remarked, as most of the meetings were run on a regular basis the agendas didn't ever change – just a list of items to be covered. He looked on the last item – the one called 'Any Other Business' – as a blessing because that coped with anything he'd forgotten.

He was finding the minutes a nuisance, as being in the chair and taking the minutes at the same time was confusing, but everybody else was too busy taking part in the proceedings. That was the theory, but he had noticed that some of them never said anything and one or two never seemed to stop. However, he looked on it as being part of the democratic process, so he assumed it was all right.

As an example of what he was talking about, Derek described the meeting he had chaired that morning. He had been ten minutes late, Mark didn't turn up and Les had to leave half-way. In spite of that, they did manage to discuss the paper that George had written and brought along to the meeting for everyone to read. It had taken quite a long time to read it and then it had to be discussed, but he thought it had probably been worthwhile.

Derek said that, as a result of having to read George's paper, the other items were rushed and the discussion about the new project had to be curtailed. However, he was rather relieved about that because he hadn't done his homework on the costings. He decided that it could be left until the end of the week when they would have an additional meeting.

The behaviour of one of the group, Greville, had bothered Derek. He described him as being in one of his funny moods. Not only did Derek find him difficult to understand when he became sarcastic, it also upset everybody else. In the end, Derek had been quite firm with him and said that he should leave the meeting if he couldn't say anything constructive, but he just sat there, smouldering.

Derek said there had been a bit of a stir when Ken accused him of having misled everyone by putting 'Welfare' down as an extra item on the agenda. Ken had thought it meant the new holiday and leave arrangements but Derek had meant the Christmas hamper for the company's pensioners, as mentioned at the last meeting. Josh then said that he thought it meant things like the proposed paternity leave, and so it went on. Derek grumbled about wishing people would look at the agendas and minutes more carefully.

Derek was very worried that the MD was going to ask about the meeting's recommendations for the appraisal system. They had spent so much time on the other things that they didn't get round to that, so he had put it on the agenda for the extra meeting at the end of the week.

He gulped down his drink and said he had to go and do the minutes while he still remembered what had happened. He reminded himself that he must put 'action' by the relevant items in the minutes and he left muttering something about hoping that everyone who said they would do things remembered to do them.

CHAPTER 3

Additional skills

There are many skills available to you these days which would probably not have been acceptable to managers of a generation ago, or which have changed over the years. Some of these would certainly give you greater control over the way in which you spend your time, and more choice in the way you wish to carry out the activities that make up your job.

Keyboard skills

One of the most important recent skills is the ability to use a computer and, therefore, a keyboard. For managers involved in scientific research, engineering or computer-related industries, this is probably not a problem, but for many managers keyboard skills are still 'just for typists'.

If you are involved in writing long, complicated or technical papers and reports, the ability to use a word processor or a good electronic typewriter is invaluable. The time saved by thinking straight onto the machine or screen is well worth the effort of learning how to use the keyboard competently. Most word processors or computers have software packages that will teach you to type, so you become familiar with the machine at the same time as learning to use the keyboard. As you increase your typing speed, you will find that writing out complicated documents in longhand becomes painfully slow since you can no longer keep up with your thoughts.

As a manager, you will not usually be expected to type and send out letters from your organization, so you will not need to know the finer details of layout and presentation. That is what typists are taught to do and is something you don't have to learn when you work at a computer, because it does all the basic work for you. If your report needs to be distributed, your secretary or the word processor operator can tidy it up for you so that it presents a good image and is easy to read.

How to be a good author

In this sense, 'author' means the person who originates a document which will be processed by a computer. There are dangers to be aware of when you know that mistakes, additions, alterations, modifications can all be dealt with comparatively easily.

The main complaint of operators is that authors are suddenly becoming so fussy about their literary efforts that they are abusing the time saved initially by doing the work on the computer. They think that all changes may be made at the touch of a button and they strive for a degree of perfection that is quite unnecessary.

It is a fallacy to think that all modifications may be made so easily. It may look like the simple depression of a key but that is not always the case. If you have a general idea of the scope of the machine, you may be more sympathetic to what it can and cannot do. Be reasonable when you are asking for text to be altered and be thankful that, if the word-processing ability is being used properly, it is saving you and your staff a great deal of time and effort.

79

Report writing

Most managers have not been trained to write. Apart from tips on how to answer exam questions, the majority of managers have been given no help at all on how to tackle the task of writing, whether reports, letters or memos. One of the activities that a manager acquires when he leaves his practical 'doing' job is that of writing about what has happened, what is happening and what is going to happen. Everybody complains about the amount of paperwork that is generated and, in spite of the present talk of the 'paperless office', it is clear that a great deal of paper is still produced every day.

When you know you have a report to write, it is best to tackle it quickly and not leave it in a pending tray until later because it won't, contrary to your wishes, go away!

You don't have to become a literary giant, a potential Nobel prizewinner (most people wouldn't read it anyway), but you do need to be clear and concise. By following a few simple rules, you can produce a document that fulfils its purpose and takes the headache out of writing it.

Am I the right person to be writing this report?
You may be the acknowledged expert on the subject, in which case gathering together the data will not present any difficulties. If you do not possess the required expertise, and no one else does either, regard this as a good opportunity to learn something new.

Do I really know what the subject of this report is?
You should make sure that you are clear what your terms of reference are. If you have been asked by someone else to write the report, check back and make sure that you are both talking about the same thing.

Why am I writing this report?
Find out why this report is needed because you will then be in a better position to get the message across. If you know the background to the subject, it will be clearer to the reader what you are saying.

Who is going to read this report?
You must be aware of the reader. If you don't know who is likely to read the report, you will not be able to present the material in an appropriate way. It is vital that you use words, illustrations and a style which are easily understood. This will vary according to the audience you are aiming at. The same subject matter may be presented in different ways to different readers. For example, the company's annual report should be presented in different ways to the board, the financial specialists, the non-financial managers, the supervisors, the semi-skilled workforce and the skilled workforce, bearing in mind that each group will have particular needs and interests.

The material: what is it? where is it? how shall I present it?
There are several ways of drawing up a plan of work for the preparation of a report, the suitability of each depending on the complexity of the paper to be produced.

For a simple report, or as the starting point for something more complicated, you could use a form of brainstorming similar to those mentioned later in this chapter.

For a longer report or one which is prepared over a long period, you may find it useful to work to a column plan like the one suggested in the Industrial Society's booklet *Communication Skills Guide – Report Writing*.

Keeping clearly in your mind the purpose or reason for the report, as well as thinking about possible conclusions and recommendations, you will now be able to select from all the data you have available that which will be used to support your arguments.

NOW can you begin to write your report?

Not yet. There is still more preparation to do which will make the whole business of writing less daunting.

What is the structure of this report?

A report is made up of several parts, and not all of those listed below will always be relevant but, until you become more confident about writing reports, it is good practice to include them.

- title page
- contents
- acknowledgements
- terms of reference
- introduction
- procedure or summary
- findings
- conclusions
- recommendations
- appendices
- bibliography/references
- glossary

What words and style am I going to use?

As I mentioned earlier, you should use different ways of presenting material according to the reader. This does not mean that you have to use a different type of English for each type of reader. You are aiming to write clearly, concisely, simply and accurately. You may be able to use technical words for some readers but you may have to explain them for others. You should not resort to jargon unless the report is to be restricted to people within your own group or business. Generally, your 'in' words and phrases will be incomprehensible to a lay audience.

As an author, you are trying to achieve readability, that is, clarity of expression, balance of ideas and arguments, and interest in what has been written. You should, therefore, keep sentences and paragraphs simple and short. It is important to break long sentences down into shorter ones rather than using lots of punctuation. If you are not sure about punctuation, try speaking the words out loud and that will usually give you a clue as to the right punctuation to use.

You will find it difficult to write well if you try to copy someone else's style. You may learn from the way somebody else writes but you will have your own style. It may just need practice to develop it and for you to feel comfortable with it.

What should the report look like?

You may be one of those people who can't be bothered with the appearance of your report. After all, you've spent a great deal of time writing the wretched thing, you don't want to be concerned with what it looks like. If you are fortunate, you will have a secretary or typist who will transfrom your handwritten pages into a beautifully presented document which is laid out with headings and sub-headings which stand out clearly, numbered if necessary and always consistent.

If your typist is inexperienced, she may not know which layout you prefer. If she is just plain lazy or uninterested (perhaps taking her cue from you?), she won't bother with presentation and you will be left with a document that is difficult to read because too much text is crammed onto a page, the visual material is untidy, and it is difficult to find your way around the information.

When should I revise my report?

If you have enough time to leave your report for twenty-four hours before revising it, you will approach it with a fresher outlook. It is difficult to be objective about something which has occupied your thoughts for some time and a breathing space is useful.

You may ask for a draft to be typed out before you revise the report. With modern word-processing facilities, it is relatively simple to do this and amend the draft without all the bother of complete retyping. The obvious advantage of revising a typed document is that it is easier to read than the handwritten version.

When you are revising the draft, review the purpose and check that it is doing what you were asked to do. Make sure that it is logical in argument and layout and that it is 'readable'.

After you have carried out a thorough revision and made any alterations on the draft, you may want to ask a colleague or friend to read through it before you send it off for the final version to be produced.

And finally . . .

When you receive the final typescript, make a final check that it is as you wanted, that nothing has been left out, and you can then submit it in the knowledge that you have carried out the task to the very best of your ability.

Writing and producing some reports can take quite a long time and therefore need careful planning. If you work backwards in time from the date the report is needed, you can begin to schedule the various stages. It is important to remember to include time for such things as: printing off the required number of pages, either from the computer or on the photocopier (and remembering to check there is enough paper!); making sure that someone is available to collate and/or bind the report; allowing time for collating and binding; thinking about how the report will be distributed, especially if it is going to external people; and, where possible, allowing some extra contingency time, just in case something goes wrong at any stage along the way.

Letter and memo writing

Most managers have to write letters at some stage during the working week. Many will try to avoid writing letters by telephoning or arranging face-to-face meetings. Some may save the time and effort of writing or dictating replies to letters and memos by handwriting an answer or comment on the original document and returning it to the author. This is a good way of dealing with internal mail which does not require a copy in the files. For instance, accepting an invitation or asking for a comment on previous correspondence does not warrant the time or money involved in dictating a formal reply.

However, there will come a time when you have to write a business letter and it is a matter of practice to make this task one that you don't view with alarm and despondency. If you follow a few simple rules, you need no longer be worried that you are presenting a bad image of the company and yourself, and need not fear making a fool of yourself in front of the person who will be typing the letter.

There are several types of letter:

- enquiries (seeking information)
- quotations (giving information)
- complaints
- adjustments (dealing with complaints)
- circulars (information and advertising)
- references and testimonials

Whatever the type of letter, it will need sound preparation and will need to follow the same basic structure.

Preparation
- Make sure you are writing to the right person and, if appropriate, find out that person's name so that you can address the letter to him personally.

85

- Make sure you find out as much as you can about how much the person you are writing to already knows about the subject and what he wants or needs to know.

- Make sure you have all the necessary support documentation such as previous correspondence, relevant files and notes in order to have all the facts you need for your letter.

- Make sure that you jot down what you need to say in a logical order. At first, you may have to write quite a lot but, as you become more confident, you will find you only have to make a list of headings to remind you of what you want to say.

When you have prepared yourself thoroughly, you will be ready to write or dictate the letter or memo. Before you call in the shorthand writer, start the audio machine or commit pen to paper, be aware of extra information you may need to ask for, mention or look for, such as unusual spellings of names, references, extra copies, urgency and priority, enclosures. Also think about how you will address the recipient of this letter. Is he 'Dear Sir', 'Dear Mr Williams', 'Dear James' or 'My dear Jim'? This salutation may well set the tone for the rest of the letter.

Identify the subject
You will need to refer to the reason for writing and you may do this by having a separate heading, by mentioning a specific event, or by a combination of the two, for example:

Dear Mr Williams

Holiday No. 354B12–Tenerife

Thank you for your letter of 19 September 1985 in which

you expressed concern at the standard of accommodation in your hotel during your recent holiday.

State the facts
It may be useful to summarize what has gone before, especially if there is any chance of misunderstanding, so that any problems may be identified quickly. You must be sure that your facts are accurate and you present them clearly and concisely:

We naturally checked immediately with our local representative in Tenerife to get an explanation from her. She has telephoned today with full details of the situation and I should like to pass these on to you.

As you mentioned, you had booked a suite overlooking the beach. When our representative checked the records she realized that there had been a mistake by the reception staff. A Mr and Mrs John Williams had checked in with the group which arrived before you and they were given your suite.

Our representative also looked into your allegations of rudeness from the reception staff when you tried to clarify the position. She confirms that one person in particular has acquired a very unfortunate reputation among holidaymakers and other staff alike.

Show the way ahead
You should now let the recipient know what action needs to be taken and who will be responsible for it.

To show our regret at these incidents, we are pleased to offer you a choice of compensation. We will either arrange a cash refund to you, reflecting the inconvenience and disappointment that you must have felt, or we will be pleased to offer you a weekend as our guests at the Hotel Splendide in Paris at any time convenient to you.

Perhaps you would be good enough to let us know which alternative you would like to accept and we will make all the necessary arrangements.

As for the rude reception clerk, he has been dismissed and we will do our best to ensure that in future our staff are more aware of similar potential problem areas.

Conclusion

Letters should end with simple, polite statements which leave the reader feeling positive and not left hanging in mid-air.

We are very sorry that you have had to write to us with these complaints but we are grateful to you for bringing these problems to our attention.

Please accept our apologies and we hope that you will use our company again for future holidays.

Yours sincerely

Reginald Lovell
Managing Director

Language and style

Most managers have now abandoned the old-fashioned business language which thanked customers for their 'esteemed order of the 12th inst' but for some people there persists the feeling that there is a special vocabulary to be used in business writing.

As the main purpose of any letter or memo is to communicate a message, avoid long flowery phrases when a few simple words will do and be as precise as you can so that the reader is in no doubt about what you are trying to say.

The tone of the letter should be appropriate to your relationship with the reader and the content of the letter. When you read through the finished document, you should be sure that you have not been too familiar or abrupt and you should be confident that it is interesting and easy to read, as well as covering all the facts.

Layout

Your organization may have a house style which is adopted for all documents. This presents a professional image to the outside world and means that everybody within the company knows what is expected. If there is a guide to layout, either as a separate document or part of the company handbook, temporary staff will be able to produce work that is in accord with the accepted house style.

If there is no overall layout for your company, you should look for a clean, well-presented document that is attractive to look at and easy to read. Secretaries and typists who have had a good training will be able to show you the different types of layout and, between you, it should be possible to choose one which will enhance the image of your firm.

Memos

Memos are generally used for communications within a company and may be written or typed on a form specially designed for the purpose.

It is not always necessary to have a memo typed. For instance, if it is only a few lines long, it may be as easy for the manager to handwrite it as to dictate it and wait for it to be typed. If a short reply is all that is needed to another memo, it is simple to jot down an answer on the original document and then return it to the sender. If you need to keep a record, you could photocopy it before sending it back.

The general rules for letter writing apply to memos,

although you do not need to top and tail them with the salutation and close.

As memos are generally written for internal use, some writers do not give as much thought to the tone as they would to letters going outside the organization. It is important that politeness and courtesy are still evident as this is part of good staff relations.

Brainstorming

At school, we are traditionally taught to take notes in sentences or vertical lists, and print on a page is laid out in a series of lines starting at the top left-hand corner, so we become used to taking notes in this way.

If you look around, you will see that we also take in information which is presented in a non-linear way. Our environment, buildings, furniture and cars, photographs, drawings and diagrams, are not neatly presented in rows or lines, and yet our minds cope perfectly well with the information.

When you need to prepare for an event like writing a letter or report, gleaning information for a proposed project, deciding where you want to go on holiday, planning your future, you probably write a neat list on a piece of paper in traditional lines.

There are other ways of brainstorming and these have been given names such as mind maps, brain patterns and pattern notes. They do not suit everybody, but you might like to try the technique next time you have a problem to solve to see if you can use it successfully.

1 Rather than start at the top left-hand corner of a piece of paper, write the main theme or idea in the centre of the page.

2 Starting from the main idea, draw lines out towards the

90

edge of the paper, each one representing a separate idea related to the central theme.

3 As you think of ideas connected with any of the branches you have drawn, include them by adding extra side branches.

4 It is important to let your mind be free, to churn out ideas in an apparently random fashion, without being restricted by worries about where they should go in a list. You will probably find that you will not have time to stop and reflect on what you are writing down because the ideas are flowing so quickly. That is good because if you stop and stem the flow of ideas, you may well leave something important out.

5 The pattern that results from this brainstorming session will probably look something like the example in Figure 8 which I drew up when I was first asked to design a time management course. It isn't very neat and some managers shy away from the technique because of this, but if they persevere they often find they can overcome their dislike of this initial lack of order.

The advantages of this kind of note-taking over the traditional linear form are:

1 The main idea is immediately obvious.

2 The most important ideas are near the central theme.

3 Related ideas and sections may be linked easily by means of arrows or circles.

4 Additional thoughts may be added quickly without having to squeeze them in between other ideas.

5 As each pattern will look different from other patterns, it will be easier for you to remember what was recorded.

Figure 8

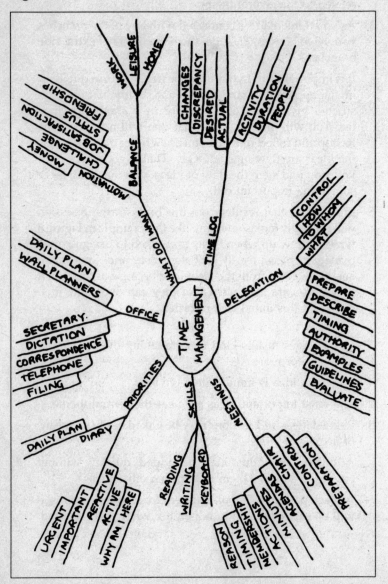

6   This technique encourages a degree of creativity which is
    not always possible in making traditional lists.

When you have finished this exercise, you will have all your
ideas down on one sheet of paper, and different topics will
have emerged as a result of being able to add to different
branches spreading out from the main central theme. If one
branch gets too large, it can be treated as a separate subject
by becoming the central theme or idea.

What to read and how to read it

When you are faced with the mountain of paper that comes
onto your desk most days, you probably think, 'I can't
possibly read all that and do the other things I have to do.'

The way we are taught to read at school is fine for that
situation, but it is not very useful for the person who has to
get through a large amount of reading quickly, without
losing understanding and retention. It has been shown by
research into reading that most people who learn the habit of
reading faster also develop greater comprehension of the
material.

There is no magic formula to help you with this. As with
most skills, it takes practice and a commitment of your
already valuable time. You will need to learn how to select
the material that has to be studied more carefully from the
articles for which you need only a vague understanding, or
the reports which require a good understanding without the
need to remember all the details.

You may be able to cut down on the amount of material
that you presently wade through by getting other people to
help you. For instance, your secretary or assistant could go
through the daily papers or many of the journals and
advertising literature that arrive regularly through the post
and earmark those passages or articles which are of interest
to you. This will save you the bother of going through papers

93

just in case there is something worth reading and it also has the added advantage of keeping your staff up to date.

For material that has to be looked at carefully, you may not need to increase your speed of reading to a great extent. It may be more important to ensure that you are able to sit comfortably in a congenial atmosphere with no interruptions so you are in a relaxed frame of mind and, therefore, more receptive to the content of the paper.

As such a lot has been written about speed reading, I don't intend to go into detail here. There are books, courses and seminars available which help identify the problems you have with reading and which offer ways of overcoming them. Most managers who have adopted these techniques find they now enjoy reading, as opposed to regarding it as a chore, and are able to read for pleasure as well as for work.

CHAPTER 4

How to manage your team

One of the results of completing the time log may well be that you realize how much time you spend with things *you* shouldn't be doing at all. You may be doing jobs that your staff should be doing, and interfering in jobs that they are already undertaking. The whole issue of *delegation* leads to some heart searching but, if you are to progress with your real job, you will have to hand over some of the tasks to other people. This can be very painful indeed. The reasons delegating can be so difficult are discussed on pages 128–34, where we also describe how the difficulties can be overcome.

As well as being reluctant to delegate, you may also face the problem that you have been promoted over some of your colleagues, so there is the psychological difficulty of trying to keep the correct balance between boss and workmate.

Study 6 depicts a young man who is facing, for the first time, the worries of heading up a team of people he doesn't know very well. It is a common situation and, as usual, there doesn't seem to be anyone around to offer constructive help.

We'll look at all the potential problems a little later, but first we should consider the subject of subordinates and think about ways of getting the right people and keeping the right people.

STUDY 6

Charles MacDonald had only recently joined the company as an advertising executive. It was his second job. Since getting his first class honours degree in economics, he had spent eighteen months working as a trainee in the marketing department of one of the giants in the pharmaceutical industry, and he now felt he knew enough about the business to become a manager.

In his new job, he was in charge of a small team of six: a secretary, two market researchers, a public relations assistant, a progress chaser and an advertising assistant.

He did feel rather nervous about being in charge of other people, and he'd never had a secretary before but, being a self-assured young man, he felt confident that he could cope. He'd always been told he was good with people so he didn't envisage any problems in that direction. He also felt that, as long as he knew what everyone was doing and he was seen to be fully conversant with all the latest trends in the advertising world, he was on the right road to being a success.

As he had his own office for the first time and he remembered hearing somewhere that a good manager is always accessible to his staff, he decided to operate an open-door policy. He noticed that the secretary was about his age and seemed to spend most of her time sitting at the desk typing or answering the phone, so he wasn't going to have to worry about her much. She'd been with the company for three years and seemed friendly enough and he wondered if he could ask her to get his cup of coffee when he arrived in the morning.

His assistant seemed to have been with the company for ages although she was only in her mid-twenties. She was obviously very competent, although Charles was getting a bit fed up with everyone saying, 'Oh, don't worry, Joanna knows all there is to know, you'll only have to ask her if there's something you don't understand.' He felt that he'd have to watch his step or Joanna would take over his job, given the chance.

The two market researchers were very experienced and had a good record within the company. Sue was married and her children were in their teens. Charles thought that, given her situation and that of the other researcher, Alan, who was a bachelor, he must be careful not to overburden her with work.

He was a bit worried about the progress chaser, young Celia. She was rather sullen and brusque in her manner and he was concerned that she might disrupt what seemed to be a good team of people. He also wondered if she spoke to clients and agencies in the same offhand way.

Jenny, the public relations assistant, gave a very good impression but Charles began to have doubts about her real ability, following remarks by his predecessor and after watching her at a meeting the previous week. As the industry was going through a period of 'bad press', he was keen that the company's image in general, and his products' image in particular, should be without blemish.

Determined that he should start off on a firm, but friendly, note, Charles instigated a weekly meeting for all members of the section on Monday mornings so that he could keep tabs on what was going on. As he had always enjoyed the excitement of a new campaign he made sure that he was in on everything. He saw the individual members of the section separately and that way they could keep him up to date on their work (except for his secretary, Debbie, because he didn't think he needed to know what happened in the office – that was her province).

He enjoyed all the contacts with the designers and the product managers because they were such a lively bunch. He thought it was useful to exchange views with people outside the section, especially as he had so many ideas. He didn't think it would harm his image to be seen to be aware of what was going on and he thought that people would expect to see him, not his subordinates. He felt sure that his staff would appreciate him taking some of the work off their hands so they could get on with other things.

How to get the right people

Managers do not always have the opportunity to interview potential members of their staff, or believe they do not have the opportunity. If someone is going to work fairly closely with you, it would make sense for you to have the final say in the appointment of that person. As a manager, you should have had a hand in the definition of the job and the kind of person who is likely to fit that description. In a large organization, a member of the personnel department will probably have written and placed the advertisement, and screened the applications so that you see only the few suitable for interview. Personnel may well carry out the first interview, allowing you to come on the scene for the final interview.

If you don't have such support services available, and have to do most of this type of work yourself, you know how much time it takes and how great is the temptation to take short cuts. I would urge you, however, to spend time on this activity as it is crucial to the future success of your team and working relationships. You must be clear about what the job is that you are hoping to fill. You should also have a good idea of the skills, knowledge and personal qualities needed for that post. It is useful to separate the essential from the desirable, and that does mean looking very carefully at what the job needs. For instance, you may think that you need a secretary who writes shorthand at 120 wpm, but do make sure that a fast speed is really necessary because, if you employ a high-speed writer and you don't use that skill properly, she will soon become fed up and leave. Try to be honest in distinguishing between what you would like to have and what you need.

The wording of an advertisement is not an easy thing to do. The ideal advertisement should bring in only two applications, with nothing to choose between them! Be as precise as possible if you are recruiting for a specific job so that you can immediately reject those people who are applying for applying's sake. You are looking for quality in applications, not quantity.

As there has been much written on the subject of recruitment and selection I won't go into detail, but it is important to get the first stages right and thereby stand a better chance of getting the right people into your team.

Interviewing is one of those skills that everyone thinks he can do. As with most management skills, it has to be learned. Some people are naturally much better at it than others, but most managers can pick up enough tips to conduct a competent interview which has a good chance of picking the right person.

Often interviewers concentrate on the professional or technical skills of the applicant. This aspect is, of course, important but there are many pointers to the ability and areas of competence of a candidate which only need to be confirmed during an interview or, if you use the system of referees, in a reference. The more difficult area to deal with is that of the person: how to assess his or her character and ability to work in a team, under pressure, as well as deciding whether you are going to get on together. Most of us do not like probing into other people's backgrounds, into what makes them tick, why they choose various options in education and work, how they have been influenced by others, and other personal details that will distinguish them from other candidates of similar ability. In our culture, we are not encouraged to delve into these private details, but it does help you to choose the right person for your team and it can be done in a gentle, sympathetic way which will not offend the applicant.

One of the main tricks of interviewing well is to prepare thoroughly beforehand. It is worth spending as much time as possible, but at least half an hour, reading the application form, getting to know the history of the candidate, keeping an eye open for any inconsistencies in dates, career choices, general interests. One of the main criticisms candidates have of interviewers is that they are not prepared for the meeting, and that they have to keep referring to the form for information they should have in their heads. I usually transfer the main points I need to cover onto a single A4 sheet, which is much easier to refer back to than a complicated, many-sided form. Any notes that I make during the interview are recorded on this sheet in a different colour, so I can easily see which points I have covered and those which are left.

The candidate should do most of the talking. The interviewer, by asking certain types of question, can encourage the applicant to do this, rather than just answer 'Yes' or 'No'. If you establish a friendly rapport with candidates right from the start, it is surprising how much they will tell you given the opportunity.

An interview should not generally be stressful. Both candidate and interviewer are in an unreal situation and to add an element of pressure is not constructive. However, if an applicant seems to be evading an issue or is not answering questions satisfactorily, you can push gently for more information or for clarification of a point until you feel sure that you have got as much as you can from that particular line of questioning. After all you, and maybe others, have got to work with this person and it is not only the professional abilities which are important, but also the personal qualities.

You will need to sell the company and the job to the applicant, but don't promise things you can't deliver. Be truthful about any difficulties that may substantially affect the job but stress the positive side, too, and give as clear a picture as possible about the company and the job.

Make sure the candidate has all the necessary information

to make a considered judgement about the job, and feel certain that you know as much as possible about him or her before you make your decision.

Interviewing for a job is only one kind of interviewing. Others include appraisal, counselling, disciplinary, grievance, and exit and, while the content is different, the approach and techniques used by the interviewer are vitally important factors in their success or otherwise.

In Study 7, the problems facing a busy manager who has to recruit a new member of staff are shown.

STUDY 7

The stores manager, David Hutchinson, was on the phone to the personnel department following the resignation of one of his young assistants, Peter. He was really fed up about having to think about getting someone new in and he asked Personnel to do whatever was necessary to find a replacement.

When they asked him for a job description, he told them that he didn't have an up-to-date one, and that they'd have to use the old one because Peter wouldn't have time to think about it before he left at the end of the week.

He reluctantly agreed that he'd have to see the shortlist, but he pleaded with them to keep it really short because he didn't have the time to interview more than three or four. He wasn't really sure why he even needed to get involved with the interviews at all. He thought Personnel could do everything and all he'd have to do was say hello and, unless he really couldn't stand the sight of the person, that would be all right.

He pointed out that it would be difficult to show applicants where they'd be working because the electricians and carpenters would be in, the carpet wouldn't be down and there was no furniture. Would it be best, he asked, if Personnel explained what was happening and not show them the space, or they might be put off?

David wanted somebody to start on the week he went on holiday. He didn't think that would matter because there was plenty for the new person to be getting on with.

How to keep the right people

Once you have selected and appointed the right candidate for the job, you then have to work even harder at keeping your new employee. Many people find that starting a new job is far more demanding than they had expected. It may be exciting and challenging, but it will also include some stress. This is because of the 'company culture', that is, the rules and code of an organization which existing members will know and generally adhere to. The jargon of that particular industry, the use of initials for people or departments, accepted custom and practice will all contribute towards a feeling of strangeness and ignorance for the newcomer. The first few weeks in a new job will colour the way an employee views the company and the people in it, and also the way the existing staff will treat him or her. Existing staff want to be able to accept a new person as quickly as possible as an effective member of the organization. They don't want someone who is a nuisance while learning or who may leave before becoming fully useful.

To minimize any risk, therefore, it is important that the process of *induction* should be successful. Induction may be described as 'the process of helping the newcomer to adjust as quickly as possible to the new social and working environment in order to achieve maximum effectiveness in the shortest possible time'.

It is usual to spend only a few minutes thinking about how a new employee will be introduced into the company. Study 8 is typical of the amount of thought that precedes a newcomer's entry into the workplace, where it is confidently expected she will spend some years of her life.

Does your company have a policy on induction? Many companies do absolutely nothing in the way of induction and others regard it as something which happens only on the first day at work. In reality, it usually starts from the moment a potential candidate reads your advertisement, through the interview and first day at work until he or she is fully conversant with the company culture and all aspects of the job.

Applicants for a job should have received all relevant details of the company and the post before they come for interview, which will convey some idea of what they are letting themselves in for. They may also have seen local and national advertising or heard of you by reputation, so will probably have built up an impression of the organization already. If you decide to offer an applicant the job, he or she should be sent details of the working conditions and terms to ensure that these are fully understood (it is amazing how much a candidate forgets after the interview!). Full and specific instructions should also be sent for the first day explaining, for example, the starting time, where to report, where to put cars or bicycles and, if the site or building is large or complex, you should include a map.

I think that the most useful way of looking at induction is to think of it as a programme into which various courses slot at appropriate times. Such a programme may last several weeks or up to a year, depending on the complexity of the work and the frequency of certain tasks.

An induction programme would probably include:

1   first day induction into the department
2   formal induction into the company
3   long-term induction into the job

1 The department

If you were the one who carried out the interview, it would be welcoming if you were the first person the newcomer saw, if only to take him or her to the personnel office who will go

105

over necessary paperwork, rules and regulations, payment of salary, and so on, and give out any relevant booklets on health and safety, fringe benefits, union dues, and the like.

The head of the department should be available to greet the newcomer. That may be you, or your boss, or your boss's boss, but whoever is in charge should be the first to extend a warm welcome to the new member of staff. From now on, the novice is going to be confused by a battery of names and faces, and it is good practice to appoint one or two sponsors who will ease the newcomer into the job and the culture. It may be the same person who will fulfil both roles, or two different people, in which case the social sponsor should meet and introduce him or her to the other folk in the department.

The other important aspect of this sponsor's responsibility is to explain the things that are part of everyday life: where the nearest loo is, what happens at tea and coffee breaks, what the procedure is for photocopying and where the machine is, where the stationery cupboard is, and so forth. At lunchtime, it is a friendly gesture if you or the sponsor take the newcomer to the canteen and make sure he or she knows where to get what, how to pay for it, where to sit and where to take the dirty dishes.

The work sponsor should soon take over to begin the process of introducing the newcomer to the job which is, after all, the object of the exercise. Most of the aspects of work induction are dealt with in Section 3: long-term induction into the job.

2 The company

The kind of formal induction given to introduce new members of staff to the company will depend very much on what level of job you are dealing with. I know one company which takes everybody, including the women on the production line and the warehousemen, on a simple half-day session finishing with lunch in a local hotel. The same company also has a one-day course for clerical and support staff and a two-day course for other managers and graduates.

The main objective of these courses is to describe what the company does, how it has evolved, its history, other sites, its products or services, and to make sure that newcomers are familiar with the family tree. Senior managers and directors are encouraged to come along, especially on the two-day course, so that they are available to answer questions and to present the company's policies.

Visits are made to different departments enabling members of one section to see how their work fits into the whole organization. It does seem to help, say, the packers if they have seen the department where the orders are processed and the works where the products are made. Members of the different departments are asked to act as guides to the visiting group, and this helps to give them a pride in their place of work as well as a deeper understanding of what happens there.

This formal course will not be held frequently in smaller companies and, in the case of the graduate intake, it may be once every four or five months, depending on the numbers involved. If you have a training department, this will be their responsibility, but it may be something that you have to organize.

3 The job
The major part of an induction programme is the introduction of new employees to their jobs and this includes any necessary training or retraining. The whole programme may take as long as a year to complete, so the initial design may be time-consuming but, once done, it will take a lot of the risk out of learning a new job. In some cases, the same programme may be applied to several newcomers, especially if the job is one for, say, management trainees, drawing office

107

staff, purchasing clerks or sales representatives where the areas of knowledge and skill are roughly the same. For one-off jobs, you may have to devise a completely new programme.

The kinds of things that may be included in an induction programme are:

- Who are the people the employee deals with regularly/not so regularly?
- Which internal departments will the employee need to know?
- Which outside organizations will the employee be dealing with?
- Which skills will the employee need to acquire – for instance, how to use the computer or calculator?
- Which meetings will the employee need to attend, chair, or take minutes of?
- Which procedures will the employee need to know – for instance, how to get dyelines printed, how to book a conference room, how to get reports typed and distributed, how to organize travelling arrangements, and so on?
- What professional qualifications should the employee be aiming for, and how does he or she go about getting them?

Against each of the categories should be set a time limit. For example, at the end of the first week, the employee should have met everybody in the department, attended one staff meeting, learnt how to use the telephone and directories, found out where the accounts and advertising departments are, and learnt how the postal system works and what the procedures are for dealing with mail.

By the end of the first month the employee will be dealing with customer queries on the phone, answering letters about supplies, will have written his or her first monthly report (this time with your help – next time alone).

At the end of six months, the employee will have spent at least one day in each department on this site, accompanied the boss to client meetings and prepared a draft costing for at least one project within the department.

And so on.

If you ensure that you monitor progress regularly through this programme, you will soon spot any problems or omissions. You may ask some people to keep a record for a few months, writing down any new task as it appears, noting its frequency and how it is to be done. This way, your subordinates are writing their own job descriptions which may highlight areas for discussion at appraisal time or whenever you carry out a review.

A departmental manual is a useful tool for reference purposes. Most companies have a brochure or something called a handbook, which is really only a list of telephone extensions and a copy of the family tree but, if it is to be of any worth, it should be a carefully compiled account of what makes the company tick. It could be the company handbook plus extra information which applies to your department only. For this purpose, a loose-leaf document is invaluable, as it is easy to update. I like to include absolutely everything in such a handbook, for example, a copy of the safety regulations, a list of union representatives, approved hotels and restaurants, how to claim petty cash, local shopping facilities, and anything else that could be useful to both new and existing members of staff.

From this chapter, you will see how much importance I attach to the process of induction. It can influence employees right from the start of their time with you and will ensure that you are getting what you want from them. It makes it easier to check that they are learning what they need to know, acquiring relevant and correct skills and knowledge as they go along. It also makes it easier for you to keep a check on whether the tasks they are doing are appropriate to the job or whether somebody else should be doing them. The formal process of induction should also be accompanied by 'inclusion', which means someone becoming an effective social member of a team or department as well as an efficient worker. For more on this, and particularly in relation to senior positions, read Bob Garratt's *Learning to Lead* in this series.

STUDY 8

Sandra Walters had been asked by her boss, Desmond Jones, to be responsible for looking after his new assistant when she started work in a couple of weeks' time. He had asked her because there wouldn't be any handover period with the previous jobholder, so he thought she might like some help getting into the job. The new girl had done similar work before, admittedly in a different type of company, but he thought that the work of financial departments couldn't vary that much.

Sandra had written to the new girl, Denise, telling her to report to her on the Monday morning at nine o'clock, the normal starting time. Desmond would be in his monthly meeting until eleven, but Sandra thought she could probably show her round the building, tell her where the loos and cloakrooms were, that sort of thing. She'd also have to meet everyone in the department and by the time they'd done that, Des would be ready to see her.

Sandra thought she had better warn Don when the new girl was coming, as she'd be working with him most of the time. He would need to clear his work beforehand to leave enough time to go through their work together. She also thought there were some company procedure manuals somewhere that Denise ought to see. They might be a bit out of date but at least they'd give her an idea of what to expect.

Personnel had probably sent out all the usual bumph about the company and who's who, so she wouldn't have to bother about that. However, they'd probably want to see her about P45s and that sort of thing, which would have to be fitted in during the first day.

Sandra had hoped to go to lunch with Denise on that first day but, as she had already promised her friend Pam that she'd go

111

shopping with her, one of the other girls would have to take her over to the canteen.

Des hadn't had time to give much thought to what Denise would be doing. As he was quite happy with the way Chris had been working, he would presumably expect her to continue along the same lines. Sandra wasn't really looking forward to having a new person in the office. It was always such a drag having to listen to all the questions and such a nuisance when they took ages to do the simplest task. Still, as she said, everybody was very friendly and she was sure they'd all do their best to make Denise feel one of them.

Delegation/working together

Perhaps the first thing to get quite clear in your mind is what exactly delegation is. It is glibly put forward as one of the solutions to easing the workload of a harassed manager, but the way in which it is often done proves that all aspects of the process have not been fully understood.

The *Oxford English Dictionary* has among its definitions:

The action of delegating or fact of being delegated; appointment or commission of a person as a delegate or representative; the entrusting of authority to a delegate.

The action of sending on a commission.

The action of delivering or assigning a thing to a person or to a purpose.

A delegate is described as:

A person sent or deputed to act for or represent another or others; one entrusted with authority or power to be exercised on behalf of those by whom he is appointed; a deputy, commissioner.

One or more persons elected and sent by an association or body of men to act in their name, and in accordance with their instructions, at some conference or meeting at which the whole body cannot be present.

These definitions mention authority, but not responsibility or accountability, both of which are vital to effective delegation.

Responsibility

When delegating reponsibility for a task to a subordinate, you are giving out a job which is part of the organization's activity and he or she will be expected to make and carry out decisions in order to achieve specified results within a specified time, using certain resources.

Authority
When you delegate authority to a subordinate, you are giving him or her the power to control resources and make changes on your behalf in order to achieve the required results.

Accountability
You can delegate responsibility and authority but you cannot delegate accountability. You will share the consequences of your subordinate's actions so, while he or she will get the blame for failure and the credit for success, you are ultimately answerable for everything that is done.

The above components of delegation may make you think that delegation is far too risky, so let us now ask the question, 'Why is delegation necessary?'

The main answer to this is that most managers do not have enough time or energy to do everything that comes within their area of responsibility. You must delegate or you will become so overworked that you become less effective as a manager and less fulfilled as a person. If your subordinates take on some of the tasks that you have been given or have been doing, you will have more time for planning, innovation, liaison with other departments, or looking at strategy.

Delegation is necessary if the skills and knowledge of your subordinates are to be fully used. The development of your staff is one of your main responsibilities as a manager and delegation is one way of making sure this happens in a controlled and useful way. It is also true that the teamwork in your department will be greatly improved if people feel they are being fully used, contributing usefully to the work of the department and therefore of the company.

What is the task to be delegated?

Delegation is not about finding some convenient person to give all the jobs you hate or find boring. Nor should it be used indiscriminately as there are times and circumstances when it would not be appropriate. It is about passing across part of your job – giving your subordinate the authority to make decisions without consulting you and giving him or her responsibility while you retain accountability. To do this, you will need to consider carefully which tasks you may legitimately hand over to someone else.

Before you delegate a task, it must be clearly defined in your own mind. It may be that you are passing on something that has been handed down to you and, unless you fully understand what is required, you are not likely to be able to explain it coherently to someone else. You may have to go back to the person who originally delegated the task to you and ask a lot of questions, but you need to be absolutely sure of what you have to do.

There are a few tasks which you should not delegate, but, happily, many of the things you are responsible for may be given to somebody else to do. I think we must assume here that you have enough competent people available who will accept delegation. The problems presented by subordinates who put forward objections to taking on extra work or by managers who cannot delegate will be considered later on in this section.

As with most aspects of management, there are times when a black or white case for delegating a task cannot be made. Sometimes it will depend on the size of the organization and how many people you are ultimately responsible for. For example, it is clear that you cannot carry out appraisals for all your department if it consists of one hundred and fifty people! You must be sure in your own mind of how far down the hierarchy you can be actively involved and at what point you pass over that involvement to one of your managers or supervisors.

Recruitment is one area which should not be delegated if you are selecting an immediate subordinate, but which may be handed down the line for those further down the hierarchy. You may well want to see prospective employees before the final decision is made but you will probably not get involved beyond that, especially if you work for a large concern. Where you have personnel specialists available, you should use them for all aspects of recruitment and selection and only become involved yourself towards the end of the process.

Most tasks to do with personnel should involve you at some stage. We have already mentioned appraisal, or review, interviews. These are a manager's responsibility and duty, but it will not be possible in a large company for the senior man to carry them out for all his employees.

Disciplinary and grievance procedures should also come into your field of responsibility. They should not occur often enough for it to become a burden to you to deal with these matters. You should be kept fully informed of potential trouble areas so that, if the matter does get out of hand, you will know what is going on. If the problem is not serious, your managers or supervisors will be able to cope and report back to you on a regular basis.

Any matters concerning salary are your responsibility but, again, if the numbers of staff involved are large, you will not be able to do everything. Other managers and supervisors will put forward recommendations to you for approval before being submitted to the necessary people.

In some companies, confidential, 'political' or sensitive work may not be delegated to anyone except, perhaps, a trusted assistant or a secretary (who will probably have to type any related documents anyway). The meanings of those three words will be different depending on the type of work

116

the organization is involved in.

Coaching or counselling of your staff, especially those reporting directly to you, is one of your major responsibilities as the development of the people working for you is absolutely crucial to the future progress of your organization.

The remaining tasks are those which may be delegated by you, and these include those jobs which you could do standing on your head. If you are particularly good at something, that is an ideal task to give to somebody else. You will have little to gain by doing it yourself and, as you are competent in that area, you should be well able to pass on that knowledge or skill to another. You will be aware of the pitfalls, the time needed to complete the task and the resources required. These are the tasks that will extend the capabilities of your subordinates and, therefore, be part of the development process.

The side of your work that is concerned with forward planning will contain tasks that may be delegated. 'But', I hear you say, 'I don't have enough time for planning, so how can I delegate anything to do with planning?'

Here we are involved in a vicious circle. You need more time to plan, but you are so caught up in minutiae and routine that you don't have time to do it and you can't, therefore, delegate any planning work to your staff. This means that you probably aren't doing your job effectively and your subordinates aren't given the chance to do their jobs effectively either. If you can break that circle by organizing yourself better, and then helping your staff to organize themselves better, you will have given yourself more time to deal with strategy, planning, future business and all the things that you should be doing.

Some of the work that you are involved in may include major chunks of fact-gathering, number-crunching, telephoning, visiting exhibitions and conferences and other

117

tasks that you need not do. If your subordinates can do all the groundwork for you, you will only have to bother with the final report, submission or whatever. Often, parts of an assignment may be handed out to others to prevent them being intimidated by having to do everything. Several people working on smaller, separate pieces of a bigger project will bring new viewpoints to it, and may help to get it done more quickly and thoroughly.

Having plucked up the courage to delegate some of your work, you have then to decide which tasks to let go. Remember that they must be interesting and worthwhile for the delegate, and don't begrudge the fact that they may be taking away something that you enjoy doing and are good at. It will free you to get on with some of that planning, report writing or reading that you have meant to do for months and will also contribute towards a more satisfied team working for you.

To whom should tasks be delegated?

It is traditional to talk of delegating to a subordinate and, indeed, I have done that in this book. In reality, however, we can delegate sideways and upwards as well, particularly if you consider delegation to be part of the wider subject of working together. Asking someone to do something for you is an everyday occurrence, at work, at home and at leisure, and does not involve only those people working under you.

How should the task be delegated?

We have already mentioned that you should be absolutely sure that you know what you are delegating and what results you want at the end of the exercise because only then can you successfully pass on the task to another.

I sometimes work with a group of design students at a

118

London college and once listened to a group of them complaining that the model shop never produced the right models for them. After a lively discussion, they conceded that the fault might lie not in the modelmakers' ability to produce models but in the students' lack of clear direction and brief.

Before you call your subordinates in to ask them to do a job, make a list of all the activities involved. Note down why the task has to be done; outline the likely timing; define the authority and responsibility involved; indicate the sort of things that will need to be included; and think about how the review and evaluation of the task will be handled. You must think about all these things *before* you see the delegate.

When you call delegates into your office, make sure they bring a notebook as they will need to make notes. This is important as we all know that we rarely remember everything we are told. The steps involved in actually handing over the task are as follows:

- make any introductory remarks
- describe the assignment
- set objectives
- indicate performance standards
- allow questions
- check understanding
- indicate authority/responsibility
- use examples or illustrations
- indicate review and follow-up procedure

You will need to obtain feedback from your delegates. It is easy to assume that they have fully understood what you have asked them to do, but you must make sure that you have covered everything so that they may carry out the assignment effectively and efficiently. You must make it clear that you support them and will be available for

119

advice, but it must also be made clear that you expect to be consulted only if absolutely necessary because you are not prepared to slowly take the job back!

I know some managers who keep a delegation checklist on their desk so that not only they, but also their subordinates, can see if they have covered all the above points when a task is being given out.

Delegation exercise

Delegation is not just a matter of handing over one of your tasks to a subordinate. It includes other management skills such as knowing your staff, their skills and abilities; being able to get across what is required of them so that they may successfully complete the task; interpersonal skills; training; and assessing performance standards.

There are four questions to be answered before you can delegate a task:

1 What is the task to be delegated?

2 Who shall I give the task to?

3 How shall I delegate the task?

4 How shall I control and monitor the delegate so that I know the task will be done well and so we can determine that the task was completed successfully?

We have already looked at the types of task that may be delegated and those which you should generally keep for yourself.

Assuming that you have someone to whom you can delegate tasks, you should be able to fit the task to the subordinate, that is, you should know your staff well enough to appreciate which tasks they can do and will enjoy doing, or which tasks may be used as part of their

120

development programme. Members of your team may have skills and interests which might be of use to you, but which you would never know about if you didn't make an effort to find out more about them. For example, your secretary may speak enough French to help you out with a telephone call to a potential customer in Toulouse, or your assistant may have an interest in sports which could be put to good use when compiling the feasibility research for a leisure centre that you hope to develop.

When you have decided who is going to do which task, you must then think about how you are going to delegate it. This preparation is one of the most important parts of delegation because you must be absolutely clear in your own mind what it is that you are asking your subordinate to do. Before you give the delegate a task, make a note of the areas you want covered so that you don't forget anything during the interview.

Look again at the steps involved in delegating as shown on page 119 and then work on the following exercise.

The office move
Your department is due to move into a nearby building in eight weeks' time and you have decided to ask your assistant to prepare a plan so that the move runs smoothly and efficiently. You have asked her to come along to your office. Write down how you would delegate this task under the headings provided overleaf.

1 Preparation

Outline the task, the reasons for it, things she will need to
know.

2 Presentation

Write down what you would actually say to your assistant when asking her to take on the task.

3 Feedback

Write down what you would say to check that she understood the task you were asking her to do.

4 *Follow-up*
Make a note of how you will monitor the task.

5 *Close*
Write down your final words to your assistant before she
leaves you to start on the task.

The following ideas are not the perfect solution because every manager will say things in a different way, but they will give a pointer towards an organized way of delegating work.

1 *Preparation*

- why we are moving
- timings
- authority and responsibility
- subjects to be included:

    change of address notices
    installation of services
    termination of services
    minimum disruption
    cost
    removal of furniture
    security
    floor plan layouts
    staff consultation
    access
    building work

- review and evaluation

2 *Presentation*

'Good morning, Sue. Come and sit down. Thanks for coming over so promptly – I know you've got a lot on at the moment, but there's something important I'd like you to tackle and I thought you'd like to get started as quickly as possible.

'Do you remember the MD agreed we needed more space? Well, we've finally been given the go-ahead to move into our new office in two months' time so we'll need to organize ourselves fairly quickly. We'll need a plan to deal with everything involved in moving us, furniture – you know the sort of thing? Will you do that, please? I've jotted down a few topics on this piece of paper and I'm sure you'll come up with plenty of others.

'You'll have the authority to contact the relevant people. I've spoken to most of them already and told them that you'll be in touch so they're expecting to hear from you.'

3 Feedback

You will need to make sure that your assistant has understood the task you have given her. It is dangerous to assume that, because she is nodding and smiling brightly, and taking loads of notes, she really knows what she has to do.

'Let's see how this will fit into your present work programme.'

'Do you know where to get hold of the floor plans?'

'You remember that Sales moved recently? You might like to have a word with Fran about how that went.'

'Who else will you need to involve?'

'Are there any immediate problems that you can see?'

4 Follow-up

Your assistant will need some guidance as to when you expect the information. She will also need to know that you will be available if needed.

'I'd like you to come back to me in two days' time with any queries or potential problems when you've had time to think the project through.'

'I'd like you to report progress to me every Monday morning until the move has taken place.'

'I'd like to see draft layouts next Monday as they will have to be agreed quickly.'

'After the move, I will expect a short report on how it went

127

so that we have a record for future occasions. It might also be useful for others to be aware of potential difficulties, helpful people and companies, and so on.'

'Please let me know if you need further help at any time.'

5 *Close*

'Well, I think that's enough to be starting with. Have you any questions now? Good. I'll see you in a couple of days then. 'Bye.'

Managers' objections to delegation

The fact is that, if you are to complete all the work that falls within your area of responsibility, you are going to have to delegate some of it. To most managers, this is a frightening and a daunting prospect and they will think of all manner of excuses for not doing it. Your first reaction is to think of all the reasons for *not* delegating, rather than look at the benefits of freeing your time to do your job. You'll think:

'It's quicker to do it myself.'

'Supposing he gets it wrong – I'm the one who'll get the blame.'

'He doesn't know how to do it properly.'

'The client expects me to be there – he won't talk to my assistant.'

You may well have good reasons for this attitude but, if you learn to delegate effectively, the potential risks will be minimized.

You will probably be scared of losing control, unhappy about giving up jobs that you enjoy doing, worried about the ability of your staff to do the work or concerned that, if your assistant does the job too well, he may take over from you.

Think for a moment of all the excuses you use for not passing on some of your work to your staff, and then think about how you could overcome some of these obstacles.

The first thing you must be clear about is that you are not indispensable. You may think you are the only person who can do a certain job to the level of perfection that you expect, but is it not possible that someone else could bring in a fresh viewpoint that may be different but not necessarily less right? The fear of competition from a subordinate is a very real one for some people but another way of looking at this is to admit that, until someone else is capable of taking over your job, you are unlikely to be recommended for promotion. It is also true that, generally, a good subordinate will move on anyway if he or she cannot reach full potential working in one area.

When you have overcome the first hurdle, that is, recognizing why you do not delegate, you can make a conscious effort to overcome the rest, slowly and deliberately, but gradually clearing the way for you to have more time to do your job and allow your staff the opportunity to grow and develop.

Probably the most common fear that managers have is that of losing control. If you know that you will take the rap for anything that goes wrong (and probably not much credit if it goes well!) you will not feel very happy about letting someone else do the work. However, if you follow these simple rules, it should not be such a traumatic experience. To summarize: you need to define the objectives of the task very clearly, set the guidelines, and indicate how the delegate's performance will be evaluated. While you are giving tasks to your subordinates, continually check that they fully understand what you are asking them to do. Often managers, if they know the person well, make assumptions about how much he or she is taking in and this is dangerous. You need to check. You will also need, at first, to carry out fairly strict monitoring of how the assignment is going. This is mainly to satisfy yourself that everything is still going according to plan and that nothing is happening that worries you. One of the managers on a course was aware that you can't keep looking over your subordinates' shoulders so he invented the term 'discreet monitoring' which meant checking from a distance – enough to keep them happy without diminishing their motivation.

You may not really know much about your delegates, what they are capable of, how well they work with others, and so on, so you are not confident in their judgement or ability to take on part of your work. The importance of knowing your staff comes in here. You have to give tasks that match their capabilities and not something completely outside their knowledge and skills.

If your staff do not have the requisite skills or knowledge to take on extra work, the answer may be training, or retraining. However, while you know this is the right approach, you also feel that it will take up too much time to instruct, train or coach your subordinates. The straight answer here is it will take time, there are no short cuts to developing people, but the investment of time now in your staff should have lasting long-term benefits. The ability to delegate more effectively should also make this period of training less difficult.

It is also becoming more usual for people to have to re-train to gain new skills as old ones become outdated or to update current skills and knowledge. As patterns of working change and develop, the idea of a career for life is less realistic now than even a few years ago. For further discussion of this, read Charles Handy's *The Future of Work*.

We mentioned earlier that you will have to try and get rid of the belief that you are indispensable. On every course I have run on time management, at least one manager has said either, 'The graveyard is full of people who thought they were indispensable', or, 'Just give yourself a fortnight's holiday and then you'll see how dispensable you are!' There are very few people who are completely indispensable and, anyway, it is a very selfish attitude to both your staff and the company if you refuse to let any of your work be done by other people. Nobody gains from such a stance and, indeed, it can have a harmful effect on the whole organization.

'Doing' rather than 'managing' is a familiar feature among managers, perpetuated by the fact that very few are offered any help in coping with change as they progress up the ranks. It is, therefore, more comfortable to stay doing the familiar things and not to risk tackling unknown and uncharted territory. It is rather sad to lose some of the old, familiar tasks but as you move on someone else will need to take the responsibility for them. You could always hang on to one or two old favourites, as long as they are not too time-consuming, but generally you should be strong and let them go. If you follow the delegation steps carefully, you need not be worried that the tasks will not be done properly and you can always monitor the delegate's work. You could also take the opportunity to look for a new interest to develop, one that is compatible with your managerial role and one which will develop you as well.

There are other reasons for not delegating and these come under the heading of personal prejudices. Most of us have preconceived ideas of what certain people are like. For example, a youngster with spiky orange hair and tight trousers must be rude, unreliable and dirty. We may believe that gays, women or blacks are not to be trusted or that someone who speaks with a cockney accent is either thick or a con man. These prejudices are amongst the hardest to overcome but once confronted face-on will, it is to be hoped, soon disappear as they are seen to be groundless.

Subordinates' objections to delegation

Of course, it is not always the boss who puts forward objections to delegating work. Sometimes subordinates will have plenty of good (to them) reasons for not accepting a task, and it is then up to the manager to deal with them. Common objections are:

'I don't have enough information.'

'I don't have enough time.'

'I don't have sufficient resources available.'

'I don't have the knowledge or skills.'

'I don't think I can do that.'

'I don't want to do that.'

'I don't want to run the risk of being criticized by the others.'

The temptation to tell the person not to whinge and to get on with the job is very great in such a situation but, unfortunately, it won't usually produce satisfactory results, so you count to ten and deal with the problem in a calm, but firm, way.

It may be that the necessary information isn't readily available or the subordinate is just not aware of where it may be obtained. In such a case, you have to find out where the subordinate has looked and then either point him or her in the right direction or, if appropriate, say that you will get the information.

Lack of time is a problem that faces everyone but when you are delegating work you must set realistic deadlines for each phase of the project and agree them with the subordinate. You may even be able to help that person with organizing his or her time!

If the complaint is lack of resources (money, equipment or manpower), look for efficient ways of keeping the project within the resources allocated to it. If additional resources really are warranted, it is up to you to try and obtain them. There is an alternative and that is to refuse to do the job if it really cannot be done properly with the allocated resources, but not many managers are prepared to do this. Another course of action might be to suggest the compromise that 'if you want Result A, we need more resources, but if you can make do with Result B we can manage with what we've got'.

We have already mentioned that training or retraining may be a way of dealing with lack of knowledge or skills. It is becoming more and more usual for people to have to acquire new skills during their working lives and the short-term investment of time and money is well worth the long-term benefits to the individual and the organization as a whole.

Lack of self-confidence may take a while to cure but, if the subordinate is sure of the support of the manager, this problem may slowly disappear. One way of building self-confidence is to delegate less complex tasks at the beginning, or to ask the subordinate to help someone else on a similar job before tackling it alone next time.

Some people are genuinely worried about what others will think of them and the work they are doing, especially if they make mistakes. This is linked in with the lack of self-confidence and here it is necessary to agree on performance guidelines during the briefing, so that at every stage of the project the subordinate knows what is expected.

There are people who just don't want the job and this means a lot of work for the manager. You must be firm (and there are many managers who don't take this stance because they want to be loved, or they're not sure of their ground) for the work has to be done and it is up to you to see that it is done. If it is possible to find projects that are of interest to the subordinate, it will be easier to sell. You may have to dress

133

up the task a little to make it attractive, but you can't do this too often as it will soon become obvious what you are doing. You may have to suggest that, if this job is done well, more interesting projects will come along in the future, possibly with a chance for advancement. There are, of course, some people who just aren't worth all this effort.

One of the most important things to remember is that once you have delegated a task, you must be available for advice but you mustn't interfere. It is very easy to discourage staff by handing them jobs with one hand and immediately taking them back with the other. You will find yourself in a vicious circle – you give out work but continually interfere and check everything, so your staff become unhappy, their work standards drop and you find yourself taking on more work.

The balance is hard to find but the more you delegate and the more confident your staff become about taking on projects, the less you will have to check what they are doing, which will give you more time to do the job you *should* be doing.

Managing your boss

Looking at the way you manage time gives you the perfect opportunity to complain about everybody else who stops you doing your job properly and to blame others, especially your boss. 'It's no good me learning to manage my time until my boss gets himself organized' is the common cry.

There is, of course, some truth in this statement, but it saddens me that so many managers give up almost before they've begun. A colleague showed me a way to try and do something about managing upwards, that is, how to have some influence over your boss.

First, note down how much time you spent with your boss last week. Of the hundred and twenty managers we have asked that question, only a dozen have said they had more than three hours a week with their immediate superior. That time was usually at the behest of the boss or because something was going drastically wrong. Almost no time at all was spent discussing the future strategy of the department, manpower planning, staff development or any of the things that should make up a large part of a manager's job.

Yet these same people expected to be able to influence their bosses in these snatched moments, expected them to be able to get a full grasp of what was happening below them, expected their staff to know what was going on in the company.

It is unlikely that you will influence your boss if you don't spend time with him. When you do make contact with him, what do you actually do?

You have to establish a personal relationship with your boss so that you may be more able to influence him. You have to raise the issues you need to discuss with him, not wait for him to call you in to talk about what's bugging him.

The same is equally true of the situation between you and your staff. How accessible are you to them to talk about important issues? Do you fob them off with statements like, 'Oh, you know how to do that – I'll leave it all to you and can you get it back to me by next Thursday?', or 'I can't see you just now, I've got a meeting. What about eight o'clock tomorrow morning for half an hour?', or 'What do you want to see me about George for? George who, anyway?'

CHAPTER 5

You and your secretary

The following section may appear out-of-date to many managers who no longer have secretaries or, indeed, any clerical support staff at all! It is true that the deployment of office staff has changed dramatically over the past few years but, at the top of the tree, where most of you will be aiming, there are still top class assistants used to great effect by executives and directors. Small businesses may also have an office manager whose role will be very similar to the one I have described below, so I'm leaving it in for future reference!

A well-trained, experienced secretary can be one of the most valuable members of a manager's team. She will make sure that all the systems in the office run like clockwork and that includes getting you to and from places, meetings and appointments on time and fully prepared. She will make sure that mail is dealt with efficiently and that if anything goes wrong, like the lights failing or the photocopier breaking down, the appropriate action will be taken to put them right.

Generally, much of this need not be your concern but the majority of managers seem to have a secret desire to be secretaries, judging by the amount of secretarial work they do. Not only are you doing work that you were not trained to do, but you are depriving a potentially valuable member of your staff of her work.

I am assuming here that, firstly, you have a secretary and, secondly, she is a well-trained, competent secretary. These two assumptions are enormous, but we shall talk later about what to do if neither of these apply to your situation.

There are many people, mostly women, who call themselves secretaries or personal assistants (PAs) when, in fact, they are shorthand-typists, audio-typists or copy-typists. This has arisen because of the lowly status traditionally given to office staff and 'secretary' sounds more important than 'typist' or 'office junior'. The term 'secretary' has been devalued over the past few years, and with it the regard for the work done by a secretary has diminished. As you should be deeply involved in the recruitment of your secretary, I think it is worth spending a few minutes looking at the different kinds of training that are available and what you should be looking for if you need a secretary. (It is also worth considering whether you really need a secretary, or are you just asking for one to show how important you are?)

There are many courses currently on the market which offer proficiency in shorthand and typing in only a few weeks. To the ignorant manager, a job candidate with 80 words per minute shorthand and 50 words per minute typing after a twelve-week course may sound like the answer to his prayer. She may be, if that is all the job demands, but does he really know what the requirements are to carry out his work competently and effectively?

Another candidate may have spent a year at secretarial college, passed innumerable examinations in shorthand, typing, transcription, commerce, secretarial duties, English and accounts and may have learnt about flower arranging and how to introduce the Archbishop of Canterbury to the Chairman of ICI, but do you really need all that from the person who is to be your secretary? The chances of losing somebody because they aren't being stretched are as great as you having to ask them to go because they can't cope with your work.

When you are recruiting a secretary, it is vital that you

137

know exactly what you are looking for and you must be honest about the requirements of the job. If you don't use shorthand and is not likely to start now, it is patently unwise to choose someone who wants to use that skill.

Shorthand, especially the so-called classic systems, is not easy to learn. It is a hard-earned skill and needs to be kept in use if it is not to go rusty. If you don't, or won't, dictate, then the shorthand writer will soon look for someone who will.

Typing is not so difficult to learn in terms of using the keyboard, but the presentation of material is something that some people find easier to acquire than others. You are not just looking for speed in a typist, you need someone with the imagination to set out a document so that it is pleasant on the eye and easy to read. Even if you move on to using word processors, the art of layout and presentation is useful, although the computer does most of the work.

The additional skills that a real secretary brings to an office are many and distinguish her from the typist. She will probably not spend most of her time sitting at the typewriter because she will be busy on the telephone, organizing meetings, conferences, travel arrangements, tackling her own tasks, such as keeping wall charts and diaries up to date, preparing papers for meetings, doing a lot of the ground work for your projects, progress chasing and generally trying to stay one step ahead of you in terms of keeping the routine of the office running smoothly and anticipating your needs. She will be diplomatic, fending off unwelcome callers and, where possible, dealing with queries and enquiries, as well as taking on tasks that will leave you free to get on with your real job. She will introduce procedures and routines into the office so that everyone knows where things are filed, where to get information, and exactly what is going on in the department.

She will know how to deal with people tactfully, whether over the phone, in person or by written communication. She will also know how to deal with you!

She will be interested in the work of the company and the part you play in achieving the objectives of the firm. And she should also be an interesting and well-informed colleague.

Many of today's women managers have come up through the secretarial route. A professional secretary has an all-round knowledge and awareness of her company that should be the envy of many of the executives. Use that knowledge to your advantage and if you have not already realized the potential worth of your secretary, have a talk with her. Ask her about the things she can do and, if she seems puzzled by this sudden interest, persevere – you may be pleasantly surprised.

You should make yourself aware of the range of different shorthand systems and secretarial examinations, especially if you are taking on someone who has only recently started work. For the more experienced person, the quality of her previous jobs will give a pointer to her abilities. If you are in doubt, ask one of the secretaries in your company what RSA III means or what Teeline shorthand is.

Most of the managers I have dealt with have not made full use of their secretaries' skills, mainly because they weren't aware of what they were. If a secretary has learnt to write business letters at college, the chances are that she's better at it than you are, because you have never been taught.

The other support staff that may be found in offices, such as filing clerks, clerical assistants, audio-typists, may also be able to contribute more to the efficient running of your department than you realize. If you called them together from time to time to discuss the administrative side of your responsibilities, not only would they feel more involved, but they would also probably be able to put forward useful suggestions and constructive criticisms. As they are involved in the day-to-day running of the office, they may well have some very good ideas as to how to make improvements.

139

Manage Your Time

Study 9 shows what happens with monotonous regularity in the offices around the country whenever a manager tries to use the resources available to him, in this case his secretary and her skills. Ask your secretary if she recognizes the scene!

STUDY 9

'Carol, can you come in straightaway? I must do this letter to Mr Everite, it's been hanging around for days and I'll get into real trouble if it doesn't go off today. No, it doesn't matter about that report – you can finish it later when we've done this letter. Oh, is it that late already? I hadn't realized. Well let's get on with it immediately, it shouldn't take too long.

'Leave the door open. I'm expecting Pete to call in with those proofs I asked for. Do you know, it's taken Publicity three whole weeks to produce that work – I don't know what they do with their time. It's costing the earth as well. Right, on with the letter. Have you got the file so that I can see what he said to me? No, I'm sure you had it last. Where? Ah, yes, now I can see it. That pile of papers is really getting out of control. I'll deal with it tomorrow.

'Right. Dear Gordon. No, sorry, I'd better call him Mr Everite until we've got this job sewn up. Dear Mr Everite, I am sorry for the delay in replying to your letter but we have been rather busy here with the Toy Exhibition. You ask about the timetable and costs for setting up a conference at the NEC for the hotel industry. Of course, it does depend on a lot of things like anticipated attendance, number of days, catering arrangements, seating and other accommodation, audio-visual equipment, and so on. Perhaps you – it's all right, Carol, I'll answer that. Hello, Jack. How nice to hear from you. Oh, I am sorry to hear that. When do you expect her to come home? Really? Please give her my best wishes. Will you still be able to make the meeting tomorrow? No, of course not. What about Mick coming instead? OK, I'll try him at home this evening – shouldn't be any problem. Fine, of course I understand. You just get things sorted out at home. Oh, by the way, while you're on the phone – have you heard anything from Mrs Wilkins about my new desk? It's been ages since we talked about it – I hope she hasn't forgotten. Well, you know what she's like – mind like a sieve! That's right, I don't think Bob's ever forgiven her for that! It's like the time we ordered . . . sorry, Jack, I've got to dash, in the middle of an important letter. Talk to you soon. Hope the wife gets better quickly. Cheers.

'OK, Carol, where were we? Mmmm, forget the bit after ''and so on''. Instead, I should be grateful if you would let me have full details of your requirements and I will then be able to furnish you with specific times and costs. Thank you for your kind enquiry, yours et cetera.

'The reference is the usual one and perhaps you ought to do a copy for that chap in Graphics. Can you make sure that goes out tonight, please? Yes, and the report, too. What telephone message? Lord, I forgot all about that – was it urgent? I'll have to leave it until tomorrow unless you . . . oh, come in, Pete, I was expecting you. I was just telling Carol here how long your lot has taken with these proofs – we couldn't get away with that sort of thing in this department, you know. No, I haven't got time to look at them just now but I'll do it as soon as possible. OK? 'Bye.

'Carol, sorry, where were we? Telephone message from the MD. Oh, yes, can you deal with that? Perhaps you could drop a memo up to him with available times for a meeting. Yes, of course the diary's up to date – except for tomorrow's appointment with Mr Telford at midday and . . . I'm sure there was something else but I can't remember what . . . I'll let you know as soon as I do. Off you go, then, and I'll see you tomorrow. No, you'll have to sign that letter on my behalf. I'm off now, you remember, the cocktail party at the new clients, mustn't be late. 'Bye.'

How to dictate

One of the most daunting tasks facing a manager, whether he is newly promoted or well-established, is that of dictating to a person or into a machine. It is difficult, and usually there is no help available to make this easier, so the following pages have been designed to take the hassle and fear out of dictation.

There are people who think that the number of shorthand writers will steadily decrease with the introduction of the new technology, and that personal secretaries are an expensive luxury and indulgence. However, there are still many shorthand writers currently working and still many being trained and, as it is a hard-earned skill, it is relevant to know how to use that skill to its best advantage.

I would like to stress again that to learn one of the classic shorthand systems is not easy and is not accomplished in a few weeks. There are fast writing systems available which are extremely useful and quick to learn, but which do have limitations; whereas the only limitation of, for example, Pitmans shorthand is the speed at which the writer can commit the outlines to paper. Many managers are not aware of the scope of shorthand and, because they have not been told what it is capable of, they do not always understand that anything they dictate can be written down in this abbreviated form. One manager recently asked me how he could get round the problem of dictating technical phrases to his secretary. When I pressed him further on this, it turned out that he thought she would not be able to write these words in shorthand. The only problem I could see was that she might be so unfamiliar with these words that she would hesitate before writing them and be unsure of them when transcribing, so I suggested that he give her a list of unusual and technical words so that she could work out the shorthand outlines in advance and, in future, she would have no

143

trouble with them during dictation and transcription.

One of the main problems with dictation is that not enough preparation is done beforehand. By that I mean that most managers don't give enough thought to what they are going to say before they call the secretary in for dictation. This obviously leads to both people's time being wasted. If you are dealing with correspondence, for instance, it is useful to jot down a few notes which outline the topics to be covered in the reply. You don't need to write down the whole answer because the notes will usually jog your memory as you're dictating. All this assumes that you can write concise, grammatical letters but, of course, this is another area where some training may be required. Most people are not taught how to write good business letters, but secretarial training usually includes this and it may be that your secretary can help you here, as long as you can swallow your pride and ask her!

A few points which may help in preparing letters are:

1 decide what to say
2 put it in sequence
3 paragraph for each step
4 immediately identify the subject
5 end by pointing the way ahead
6 use simple, short sentences
7 use punctuation to help understanding
8 use simple words and few of them

Your secretary will probably be able to sort out any grammatical errors, unscramble the mixed 'I's' and 'We's', and make sure that the close ties up with the opening, for example, 'Dear Sir' is followed by 'Yours faithfully' and 'Dear Ian' is followed by 'Yours sincerely', so you needn't worry too much about these to begin with.

Try to put aside set times for dictation sessions and, where possible, don't make them too long. Avoid giving work late in the afternoon, especially if it has to go out the same day. Try to make sure that you will not be interrupted during dictation. If the phone goes, ask the secretary to answer it, saying that you will call back in a few minutes, and get back to dictating. Have all the necessary files and documents readily available and give any relevant supporting material to the secretary after each item has been dealt with. It is useful if work which is to be given priority is dealt with first. Give instructions if there is anything special about a piece of work, for instance, if it requires a special layout, if extra copies need to be made or if a name has an unusual spelling. (If you have a good secretary, you may not have to give any of these special instructions but you will need to find this out if, for example, you have only recently taken over this job or if she is new to the job.)

When you are sure that you are fully prepared for dictation, you may begin. Speak clearly, without shouting, and try not to walk around the room while you are dictating. I know of one secretary who became so cross at her boss wandering round the office, as it meant she couldn't always hear what he was saying, that one day she picked up her notebook and followed him round the room. This soon cured him of the habit! Try to speak at a steady speed and at a reasonable speed. Some shorthand writers can take down at very high speeds but in the normal course of business this is not usually necessary, so speak at a speed which is comfortable for both of you. It is said that the average speed of dictation of British businessmen is just over 50 words per minute, which is very slow, but that's probably because they are not properly prepared.

When work is returned to you for signature, you shouldn't need to read it through for mistakes but, if you do spot an error, just mark it in pencil in the margin and, generally, it can be corrected easily. If you mark it in ink, the whole

145

document will have to be typed again and this is obviously a waste of time, effort and money. This applies only if your secretary is using a typewriter. Word processors will be able to deal with corrections before a new copy is printed off.

Dictating to a person is difficult, especially when you have an irrational fear of looking incompetent or stupid in front of that person and, for this reason, many managers prefer to use a dictating machine. If you can't see the effect your dictation is having on the listener, perhaps you don't worry about it so much, but I think it is even more difficult to dictate into a machine. At least, when dictating in person, you can establish a rapport and, if the relationship is good, you can alter things easily, ask for help or add in afterthoughts. A machine cannot cope with these things so easily, nor do managers realize the effect their changes are having on the audio-typist. As with most managerial tasks, some thought should be given to this activity beforehand – don't just rush at it or treat it as trivial.

Some points to remember when dictating into an audio machine are:

1 Try to deal with your correspondence in small batches.

2 Deal with three or four items on one recording at a time.

3 Plan what you want to say before commencing dictation:

assemble the facts
be clear about the content
select the right approach
prepare a plan

4 Make headings to aid an easy flow of dictation.

5 Precede any instruction with the words 'Typist, please . . .' (or even better, use the name if you know it).

6 Indicate verbally if correspondence is urgent at the start of dictation.

146

7   Make sure you give instructions about the number of copies required (and colours of copies where relevant).

8   Inform the typist of any special layout.

9   Mention the length of your dictation (short, medium or long).

10   Say whether the correspondence carries enclosures.

11   Say whether there are any files to be matched up with the recording.

12   Have all correspondence and files within easy reach.

13   Don't clutter up your desk with unnecessary papers during dictation.

14   Choose simple words, use simple sentences and have one idea to the paragraph.

15   Speak in a natural voice.

16   Not too slow, not too fast.

17   Don't shout or whisper.

18   Speak with feeling and emphasis.

19   Be precise because the machine can't ask questions.

20   Speak as if the typist were sitting opposite you.

21   Don't get the I's and We's mixed.

22   Make sure that the close ties up with the opening, as in 'Dear Sir/Yours faithfully', or 'Dear Mr/Yours sincerely'.

23   Spell difficult proper names and addresses, and use the phonetic alphabet to distinguish between difficult letters such as B and P, or T and E.

24   Dictate paragraphs and full stops, although other minor punctuation may be left to the typist.

25   Alter any corrections in pencil, so that they may be done without retyping.

Presentation of work to be typed

So many managers are reluctant to give dictation that they must submit any work to be typed in manuscript form. If you have a look at the last piece of work you handed in for typing, can you honestly say that you thought about the person who was going to have to work from that manuscript? The chances are that the handwriting was not always legible, that there were crossings out and insertions scribbled somewhere at the end or on the back of another sheet, and that you left it on the typist's desk without clear instructions or just threw it at her saying, 'Oh, the usual, please.'

When most managers are tackled about their appalling handwriting, they just grin and say, 'I know, it's awful, isn't it?' as if they were proud of the fact. It is inexcusable to hand in work that is not easily read. I know several secretaries who now give back untidy, illegible documents and refuse to type them until they are in a reasonable form.

No one minds a 'cut and paste' job as long as it is clear just what is required by the writer. However, blobs and wandering arrows, scraps of paper and light-coloured pencils, indecipherable technical words and indistinct alterations show a complete lack of consideration for the poor soul who is meant to make sense of this concoction.

Next time you submit a report or letter for typing, ask your secretary or the wordprocessing supervisor if it is acceptable or if there is any way that you could improve your manuscript work for the future.

Accepting completed work

I have stressed the importance of giving out work in an organized, tidy way but there is, of course, another side to the coin.

How often do you receive typed work back that you have not been satisfied with but have just accepted? You may have altered any mistakes yourself or put in a little postscript saying, 'Sorry about the typing, but the temp isn't used to our ways yet!' So often it's easier to put up with badly typed or presented work rather than rock the boat, get a bad reputation among the typists, or simply because there isn't time to get it retyped.

It is not difficult to learn to type and there is no excuse for poorly typed work, especially in today's modern offices with all sorts of sophisticated machinery and typing aids. If you are not happy with the final product, you should send it back until it is right. You may not be popular at first, but it is good to have a reputation as someone who likes things done properly. That way everyone knows where they are, money and time are saved and the whole organization looks more professional.

If the company does not have an accepted house style for typed documents, you should decide how you want your work presented and often a secretary can help with typing style. She may be able to compile a guide to remind her and to help any temps or assistants who are expected to do work for you.

You may well have arguments about punctuation and spelling with some secretaries. Those who have had a good all-round training will be pretty reliable in these matters and, anyway, a properly trained secretary will always have a dictionary close to hand and she won't be ashamed of using it. If she questions your writing style sometimes, just have a look to make sure that you aren't being pedantic, that you are writing the report in the best possible way.

Just because you are a manager doesn't mean that you can automatically write first-class business letters and reports. If you find them difficult or you suspect that they could be better written, find out about the short courses available at

149

your local college or maybe your own training department could run some in-company sessions. There are also some excellent short and easy-to-read books on the market which you might find helpful.

CHAPTER 6

How to organize your office

Managing an office, its staff and what goes on there, is not as easy as many new managers imagine. For some, it is a whole new way of life, using completely unfamiliar machinery, terminology, procedures and routines. Well managed, it can make the manager's job run smoothly, but a badly organized office can mean misery if letters and documents are misplaced, if telephone messages aren't passed on, if the typist won't check her work and nobody ever knows where anybody else is.

The office is one of those areas that you are meant to automatically know about when you become a manager. You may never have had a secretary before, had to worry about the pros and cons of shorthand over audio- or copytyping, or be concerned about how the mail is dealt with, both incoming and outgoing.

You may not be involved in any detail with much of the work that is done in the office, but you should be aware of the scope of operation and how useful it can be in organizing your life at work.

The specific use of secretarial and other skills has been discussed in the previous chapter, but here we will look at the everyday routines and systems of an office that go unnoticed if everything is working well but cause misery if they have not been well thought through and implemented.

Office equipment

With the good electric or electronic typewriters and word-processing packages currently on the market at reasonable prices, or even reconditioned machines at low prices, it is inconceivable to me that some companies still have manual typewriters as the rule, rather than the exception. I know of some very wealthy, well-known companies in the electronics industry where the majority of typists and secretaries have to work on second-rate manual machines. In such a case, not only are the typists disgruntled but the image presented to the outside world is not a professional, up-to-date one.

Other office equipment and furniture should be appropriate to the type of work that is being carried out, and acceptable to the people having to use them. Getting the right chairs, for example, for operators who are sitting down in front of machines for most of the day, is of paramount importance if they are not to damage their health.

A few years ago, there was a lot of discussion about the introduction of the new technology into offices. Some companies threw a lot of money away by buying equipment that wasn't suitable. A great deal of thought has to go into the selection and purchase of this type of equipment. It is not enough to look at some brochures, get the rep in and place the order. If you want a new machine or system to be accepted, you have to look not only at its suitability for the job but also at where it will be placed, who will be operating it and what the implications will be for everyone involved. A lot of time can be saved if technology is introduced thoughtfully into an organization, but it can't happen overnight.

Incoming and outgoing mail

The size and complexity of your organization will have a bearing on how involved you get in this side of office routine. Even if you are not directly concerned, you might like to show this section to your secretary or whoever is involved.

Incoming mail

You cannot blithely assume that the post is going to arrive first thing in the morning and that you will allocate some time when you first arrive in the office to deal with it. In many companies, the mail finally comes through later in the day and this makes it more difficult to deal with complex issues which require immediate responses. However, all is not lost and if you put aside some time in the afternoon as a matter of course, you should be able to cope with the most urgent letters.

If you are fortunate enough to have a competent secretary or assistant who deals with your mail, she will open it, and sort it into piles, for example, letters and other documents requiring an answer, information only copies, reports to be read, journals and articles to be scanned, and any junk mail.

You may have a system for recording all mail coming into your department, giving the date, originator, subject matter, initials of person who will deal with the letter, and perhaps a file name, number or reference. (The latter can be important because, even if it is filed in the wrong place, at least you will know where to find it!) An example of such a sheet is given in Figure 9 (page 156).

In some organizations where the principle of 'open government' is practised, all incoming mail is put into a central tray for half a day so that everybody in the office can scan through it and get an idea of what is happening. When the appropriate person has replied, the original letter, together with a copy of the answer, is put back into the central tray before being filed. This has advantages in keeping everyone in the picture but is not so efficient if someone is out of the office for any length of time. I can well understand that some managers would feel very nervous about adopting this system. All I can say is that it works very well in some architectural practices I know.

Some managers like to open their own mail, believing that it gives them a better feel for what is going on in the department. This is all right if you don't have someone else to do this chore, but it is a waste of your expensive time if there are others who can do it for you.

In most companies, it is usual to reply to internal memos with another internal memo. One way of avoiding this is to add a handwritten note to the original document and return it to the originator. Sometimes you may have to copy the document to keep a record of your reply, but often this is not necessary. Obviously, there are occasions when longer responses are required, but it can be time-saving not to have to dictate a reply and wait for it to be typed. (It also saves on the cost of stationery.)

All mail should have some action assigned to it as it arrives on your desk. Try to avoid a 'pending' tray as this, like the ubiquitous 'miscellaneous', is an invitation to lose documents for ever.

If you have a system of allocating priorities to your work, for example 'A', 'B' or 'C', depending on urgency and importance, you should mark each document accordingly and amend the list in your diary or daily plan. You may keep them in a concertina file, in a tray on your desk or in folders, but keep the top priority work in sight to minimize panics later on.

If you have a secretary, she will probably deal with all mail marked 'personal' or 'confidential', but if not, you should make it clear that they are not to be opened by anyone but you. A secretary will also be able to deal with some of the mail herself and you will have to agree, in discussion with her, whether you need to see any such mail before she answers it. Over time, you will build up a rapport with your secretary which means that she will know what she can do on your behalf and what she needs to talk over with you.

Outgoing mail

There will be times when you need to check documents before they leave your office but, generally, you should be able to entrust your secretary or assistant to deal with them.

You may have a system of recording outgoing mail similar to the one used for incoming mail. It is not always necessary to have such a record but you may find it useful for, say, showing how much is being spent on postage. A loose-leaf sheet like the one shown in Figure 10 could be adopted (page 157). If your organization has many different projects, each with a budget, it may be helpful to have separate sheets for each project so that running costs are easily identified.

All recording systems, such as the ones suggested for incoming and outgoing mail, take time to initiate. At first, they may feel awkward to complete but, generally, they are worthwhile and, as with most systems, once you are in the habit of doing them, they take up very little time and effort. As records, they are useful if one of your staff has to deal with somebody else's work during holidays or sickness. You know where to go to check if documents have been received or sent out without going through the files. When a project has been completed, the relevant sheets can be archived, along with all the other papers.

As with all systems, if they are completed conscientiously every day, they will become useful aids and not frustrating chores.

Filing

Possibly the most boring subject in the whole world! I am surprised at how often it is brought up as a problem area by senior managers whose best-laid plans are disrupted because

Figure 9

Incoming Mail			Date:		
From	To	Subject	Dealt with	File Ref	No

Figure 10

Outgoing Mail				Project no:	
Date	From	To	Ref	Subject	Cost
				b/f	
				Sub-total	
				c/f	

documents have been filed in the wrong place, or not filed at all. Filing is generally your secretary's job, or the filing clerk's job, but it may be yours if you don't have staff working for you.

There are two main points about filing. First, keep the system as simple as possible and, second, make sure the filing is done every day.

There are dozens of filing systems on the market, each with its own seductive features, but don't be tempted into something which is not going to do what you require. You may have inherited a system that undoubtedly suited the previous owner, but which may not work for you. It takes time and effort to introduce a new system or modify an existing one. However, if the present one is too complicated for other people to understand, it may be worth bringing in a new one that everybody will be able to use. Ideally, there should be some uniformity between the systems used in an organization, whether in individual departments or in a centralized filing room. However, this is not usually the case and if a manager moves from one department to another he generally finds that papers are filed in a completely different way and he has to learn a new system.

The key to successful filing is to keep the system as simple as possible. I won't go into all the different kinds of trolleys, cabinets, folders or drawers as they can easily be seen in your local stationery store or in a catalogue, and your choice will be dictated by things such as space available, security requirements, colour or cost. Don't attempt to choose the equipment on your own if you have a secretary who can help you. If you don't have a secretary, borrow somebody else's for a couple of hours!

Alphabetic, subject, geographical and numerical are the main ways of filing, or you can use any combination of the four. You could also colour code files. For example, if you are dealing with five sales areas, each region could be given a different colour and you would know that all green files related to customers in, say, Ireland, whereas the blue ones concerned Scotland, and so on.

It is best to keep individual files small, with clearly marked subsections within each major category. For example, if you were dealing with professional bodies, the files might look like this:

1.00 INSTITUTE OF PERSONNEL MANAGEMENT

1.10 Correspondence

1.11 Membership
1.12 Subscription

1.20 Meetings

1.21 Agendas
1.22 Minutes
1.23 Reports
1.24 AGM

2.00 INSTITUTE OF PUBLIC RELATIONS

2.10 Correspondence

2.11 Membership
2.12 Subscription

2.20 Meetings

2.21 Agendas
2.22 Minutes
2.23 Reports
2.24 AGM

and so on. Numbering files in this way means that you will have a uniform system within the office without sacrificing flexibility. You will know that all matters to do with sub-

Figure 11

Absent Sheet			
File name/number	Date taken	Taken by	Date returned

scriptions will have the .12 reference and this will make them easier to file and find again.

The different ways of filing are covered in numerous books on office practice and secretarial duties and will show you how flexible, yet simple, a system can be.

The other important point about filing is that it should be done every day, without fail. Once you leave it – 'Oh, I haven't got time to do that just now, I'll do it tomorrow' – the pile of papers begins to mount up and before you know it, you have two hours of filing to do! Give yourself a few minutes at the beginning or end of each day and the job will be done quickly and painlessly.

If a file is removed from the cabinet, it is a good idea to insert some kind of reminder of who has that file and when it was taken out. In offices, one of the most common reasons for delay and frustration is when you find that a file has been taken away, no one knows where or by whom, and you have to go on an expedition to find it.

An easy way of dealing with this is to have an absent sheet or something similar which records who has taken the file, when, and the date it is returned. A card or sheet attached to the front of each pocket is quickly completed, and may look like the example opposite.

It is useful to keep an up-to-date index of your files, either in front of the filing cabinet or in some other easily accessible place. That will help others looking for files who do not want to rifle through all your filing cabinets.

If you work in an office where contact with outside organizations is important and frequent, you will need to keep names, addresses and telephone numbers close at hand. There are many index systems available which enable you to keep such information on a card or strip in a box or folder on your desk or on your computer database. These are easy to keep up to date and are invaluable as a source of information.

There is no mystical side to filing – it is a mundane and routine task which, if kept under control by regular, daily attention, no longer assumes an importance which it does not deserve.

Concluding remarks

As a follow-up to the Personal Effectiveness courses I run, I always try to organize a review course which usually lasts for about half a day. Part of the exercise is to review what participants have achieved during the weeks since they were on the course, and we compare what they have done with what they said they intended to do in their action plans.

Most people make long lists of the things they would like to do and, when we review those lists, we usually find that some of the good intentions have fallen by the wayside. I am always delighted, however, with the positive things that come out of the courses.

I have chosen some examples to show what can happen once you get into the habit of organizing yourself and those who work with you.

George was a quiet, shy man who knew he was a good engineer but was having difficulty adjusting to being a manager of a large section. He admitted that he felt he didn't know what was going on among his staff and he didn't know how to give his work the correct priorities. His action plan at the end of the course was ambitious, and at the review session he told us that in the intervening six weeks he hadn't been able to implement everything, but that something he hadn't originally planned had worked very well:

I've put half an hour aside first thing each morning in

my diary for a 'walkabout' through the department. This means that I've got a better idea of what's going on; we can clear up small things without my people having to make a special journey to my office; we make specific appointments when they need to see me about something important; I can maintain the social side of our relationship much better; and because I'm around so regularly, they don't see me as the distant boss figure – it's proved invaluable.

The emphasis given to delegation on the courses proved to be justified and many managers reported back improved relationships with their staff as a result of better delegation techniques. Typical of the reactions is this one from Alan, who had decided to look at the way he gave work to his people as his first priority:

I've made a real effort with delegation. I still can't always let go completely, but things are definitely improving. I'm briefing people better and encouraging them to ask me lots more questions when I first give them work so they don't have to keep coming back. The reaction of my staff has been very favourable – they feel they know what they're meant to be doing at last!

Pam said that she had always had difficulty in deciding what she should be doing each day because she usually had a go at everything. That meant that some things were done well, but most were tackled only superficially and she worked far too much overtime. Her action plan had been very short – whereas most people aimed to do too much, she didn't have high hopes of achieving anything significant. To her, and my, delight, the review session revealed some real progress:

I've managed to keep up the daily plan – much to my own surprise – and it really has taken a weight off my shoulders, even if I only manage to cross off one item at the end of the day. I've managed to get my people to accept the fact that when the door is open, they can come in but when it is shut, they must stay out. The office seems to be running much more smoothly now, mainly because I'm using my secretary more effectively. We use the diary more and the new call-forward system has worked a treat. I'm also aware that I'm running meetings more effectively.

There are, of course, always those people who are convinced that they will never be able to put any of my ideas into operation. These sceptics think that even if they did try to make some of these techniques work, other people would stop them being successful. My delight is the greater, then, when someone like Ken comes to a review session and says:

I've been amazed at what I've managed to achieve in the past two months and my staff are pleased, too. I've begun to question my attendance at meetings; I've taken groups of people off site for a few hours to crack a difficult problem; I talk to my people more; I've looked at my subordinates' jobs and made some changes with their agreement; and I've kept to my daily plan with a creditable amount of success.

Many of the participants resolved to spend more time getting to know their staff so they could help them develop and grow into their jobs. Alison, an extrovert character who admitted that she didn't suffer fools gladly, wanted to improve relationships with the people in her group:

I'm involving myself much more with my staff and personnel matters, and I've been able to do that because I'm letting my secretary take over a lot of the stuff I used to do. We're looking at the use of space in the office, the

165

layout and so on to see if we can organize that for better communications between our group. I'm also in the middle of designing some work packages for my people, especially the newcomers, so that they have a proper induction into the section.

One of my favourite remarks came from a senior manager who was working very long hours on a project that had seen many difficulties over the past few months. Peter had resolved to delegate more effectively and to look closely at the way he planned his day. He managed to get these two targets well underway and one of the most satisfying things I have heard at these review sessions was when he said:

I now leave the office by six o'clock which means I can read a bedtime story to my little boy.

How can managing your time more effectively make you a productive member of your organization?

- By delegating certain tasks to others, you will be freeing yourself to spend more time on activities which will be of benefit to the organization. For example, planning ahead, planning campaigns and strategies, giving yourself time to think about the issues that help achieve the objectives of the organization for which you work.

- By giving the people in your team more responsibility, you will be developing them. This will not only be of great benefit to you personally, but will also ensure that the organization gets the most out of its employees.

- By constructively questioning the need to hold or attend meetings, you are making other people think about whether issues may be dealt with in other, less time-consuming, ways.

- By organizing yourself and your team, you will become an example which others in the organization may wish to emulate.

Managing your time more effectively will also enable you to look at what other things you want to do, outside paid work. To develop yourself, both at work and in your leisure time, is something you owe yourself, your family, your friends and your colleagues.

ACKNOWLEDGEMENTS

Although much of what is written in this book is the result of personal experience, trial and error, there are several people, books and films I would like to mention specifically as having been particularly helpful over the years.

Thanks are especially due to the companies, particularly Plessey Radar, Marconi Underwater Systems Limited, CASE Communications plc, C. T. Bowring, Voluntary Service Overseas, City University, Hatfield Polytechnic, The Housing Association, Upjohn Limited, Hutchison Whampoa and Hong Kong Polytechnic, who have allowed me to run Time Management courses for their managers, and to those managers from whom I have learnt so much. To my bosses in my previous life as a paid employee I should like to express gratitude for showing me such a variety of management styles, and to my colleagues from AMED, whether as sources of information or as co-trainers on the courses, thank you for your friendly help, so generously given. I have to thank Bob, my husband and editor, for so many things but, on this occasion, for having the courage to let me write this book and for being an ever-present example of someone who seems to be able to organize his life beautifully.

Some of the books I found useful are: *Use Your Head* by Tony Buzan (BBC); *Managers and Their Jobs* by Rosemary Stewart (Macmillan, London); *The Nature of Managerial Work* by Henry Mintzberg (Harper and Row, New York); *The Effective Executive* by Peter Drucker (Heinemann and Pan, London); and several publications from the Industrial Society, including those in their 'Communications Skills Pack'; the Kogan Page series, *Better Management Skills*, has some excellent short, punchy books which cover a wide range of relevant topics.

There are three films that I like to use during the Time Management courses and the review session, and they are all from Video Arts: *The Unorganized Manager* (Part 1 – Damnation, and Part 2 – Salvation); *Meetings, Bloody Meetings*; and *More Bloody Meetings*. They all have very useful accompanying booklets.

INDEX

What is AMED?

AMED is an association of individuals who have a professional interest in the development of people at work. Our membership is exclusive to individuals. AMED's network brings together people from industry, the public sector, academic organizations and consultancy.

The aims of the association

- to promote best practice in the fields of individual and organizational development

- to provide a forum for exploration of new ideas

- to provide our members with opportunities for their own development

- to encourage the adoption of ethical practices

Benefits of membership

- an extensive network of contacts

- regional groups spanning the UK and Europe

- shared experience of working on leading-edge issues

- local meetings and special interest networking activities

- a programme of national conferences, workshops and seminars

- a regular AMED newsletter and a quarterly journal

- a membership list and consultants' directory

- discounts on publications and professional insurances

- a national voice on development issues

Registered office:
Association for Management Education & Development
21 Catherine Street
London WC2B 5JS
Tel: 071 497 3264   Registered Charity No 269 706

Titles in the Successful Manager series

All these books are available from your local bookseller or can be ordered direct from the publishers.

To order direct just tick the titles you want and fill in the form below:

Name: _____

Address: _____

_____

Postcode: _____

Send to: HarperCollins Mail Order, Dept 8, HarperCollins*Publishers*, Westerhill Road, Bishopbriggs, Glasgow G64 2QT.

Please enclose a cheque or postal order or your authority to debit your Visa/Access account –

Credit card no: _____

Expiry date: _____

Signature: _____

– to the value of the cover price plus:

UK & BFPO: Add £1.00 for the first and 25p for each additional book ordered.

Overseas orders including Eire, please add £2.95 service charge.

Books will be sent by surface mail but quotes for airmail despatches will be given on request.

24 HOUR TELEPHONE ORDERING SERVICE FOR
ACCESS/VISA CARDHOLDERS –
TEL: GLASGOW 041-772 2281 or LONDON 081-307 4052